THE GOSPEL
according to
MADISON AVENUE

THE GOSPEL
according to
MADISON AVENUE

RAY HUTCHINSON

THE BRUCE PUBLISHING COMPANY / NEW YORK

Library of Congress Catalog Card Number: 74–76420

Copyright © 1969 THE BRUCE PUBLISHING COMPANY

Made in the United States of America

TO THE LATE JOHN JOLIN, S.J.

WITH DEEP LOVE AND GRATITUDE

AND PROFOUNDEST APOLOGIES

"Just as soon as the Spirit of
truth shall come, he will guide you to all truth."
—John 16:12

Introduction

Advertising reads for all the world like a secular Scripture. By chapter and verse it recounts a philosophy and a view of man, a body of sacred doctrine and a cosmology, heroes and villains, history and myth. Like the Old Testament it consists of a mishmash of songs and stories, speeches and wise sayings, poetry and prose. It is, by turns, romantic, picaresque, bizarre, violent and humdrum. Its adventures range from low comedy and hot-lipped Ur-sex across an incredible void of tedium, all the way to exalted, if mercantile, sanctity. And like that other Scripture it has of late been a kind of no-man's-land in which its Darrows and William Jennings Bryans have squared off against one another, the latter calling it the inspired and infallible word of a free-enterprise economy, the former, a useless and even damaging synthesis of fairy tale and bunk.

To say that both sides have overshot the mark would be a truism—and therefore true. You can call advertising an American art form or an incitement to ghetto looting. You might be partially right in either case. Are its dogmas canonical or apocryphal? Probably both. Praise it as a billboard of genius or condemn it as a censorial force that is driving truly talented writers clean out of television.[1]

[1] See "TV's Disastrous Brain Drain," by Dick Hobson, *TV Guide*, June 15, 1968, pp. 6–10.

There is evidence to support either thesis. Some critics say it distorts our society; others (like McLuhan) call it a "most faithful" reflection of all we stand for. This latter thesis is difficult to prove, if only because advertising copywriters, unlike those more admired evangelists, Matthew, Mark, Luke, and John, are not *common* enough to paint an accurate picture of our culture in their commercial gospel.

What are we left with? This: advertising is a human, that is, faulty, technique for selling goods that plays a useful role in our economy. In saying as much, I disagree with those critics who suggest it is a social waste, serving only to increase prices and to divert money from more important areas such as education and urban rebuilding. It is also expensive (over $3 billion for TV ads alone in 1968). I have heard professors of economics prove that Uncle Sam is paying half the tab for all advertising. If that be true, then we had better take a good look at what we (the taxpayers) are spending all those billions on and try to find out whether we are getting our money's worth.

A further note. The word "advertising" as used in this book will signify at times the paid variety of ad and at times that broader pitch by which colleges, unions, political parties, churches, etc., attempt to create an image and sell their point of view. For centuries they have courted our assent and our allegiance by the use of promotional propaganda. Since their experience far outweighs that of the infant ad industry,· the lessons they have learned can save advertising men from making similar calamitous goofs. Goofs? Yes indeed, but not because some particular "sell" didn't work. What we shall be concerned with is whether advertising is true, or honest, or ethical.

Shortly after I began this little opus, an acquaintance asked me to edit his master's thesis on business ethics. It was a deeply traumatic experience and very nearly persuaded me that another book on ethics, whether for advertisers or anyone else, would be, in the words of an old professor of mine, "a work of supererogation." Who needs it? I must admit that business as an academic discipline presents to my dumb stare an almost opaque surface. Abstractions like social responsibility scale, technical rationality, demand expansibility, and polled interdependence, along with pallid verbs like quantify, maximize, and minimize (big favorites!), do not enhance its image. I was reminded of an old German proverb: *Gegen die Dumheit kämpfen die Goetter vergebens*. The Gods do indeed strive in vain against ignorance, in this case my own.

But since my instincts have never been altogether trustworthy, I ploughed ahead, making one important decision: this book would be as unlike a textbook or thesis as I could make it. It would be written by and for the man who has never read the *Harvard Business Review,* who makes little sense of C. Wright Mills or A. Dudley Ward, but who does read newspapers and watch television and experiences vague but acute discomfort from some of the advertisements therein. The book is also designed hopefully for other, bigger fish in that opulent aquarium called "Madison Avenue," with the conviction that those fish are feeling some distaste for the medium in which they swim and would like to freshen up the water but don't know how.

Something is wrong with advertising, just as something is wrong with society, and in fact with man himself. A Christian would mention original sin at this point. But the illness need not be terminal if certain remedies are taken. Since Christ bequeathed extraordinary insights into the nature of man and his meaning, it follows that "Catholic advertising" should possess singular integrity and is singularly guilty if it does not. I put the term "Catholic advertising" in quotes because it sounds so damned possessive, like Catholic trousers or Catholic hurricanes. But I don't mean by it only advertising that appears in Catholic newspapers and magazines. I mean all advertising which pretends to be responsible and to reflect an image of man as a sacred creature whose dimensions reach beyond a purely material realm.

Prime Minister Sir Stanley Baldwin of Great Britain remarked of aviation in 1935, "I wish for many reasons it had never been invented. We must Christianize it." Many critics today feel the same way about advertising. But just who will put it right? A woman whose son was going the hippie route wrote to Abraham Ribicoff when he was Secretary of Health, Education and Welfare, "Mr. Secretary, when are you going to solve my problem?" Unhappily we are often like that mother. We glare at shoddy, insulting ads and wonder when the government will do something about it. But it never will because it never can, any more than it can change the nature of man or make him good. Only we can do something about it.

As the crisis deepens, wrote Richard Weaver, apathy mounts.[2] How true! During March of 1958 France was threatened by crisis. While the Fourth Republic teetered, Parisians set two records: for the number of motorists leaving the city on week-end jaunts to the country, and for the number of people (44 per cent) who didn't bother to vote in a by-election. It is my hope that this book will help a little to keep apathy away and with it the crisis in which advertising, and perhaps civilization in general (if you can believe Walter Lippmann), finds itself. If I can make you more sensitive to the illogic and unrationality of much advertising, if I can change your shopping trips into exercises of intelligent choice, then my book will have done its job. Let the business journals say what they will.

San Diego, Calif.
July 14, 1968

[2] Richard Weaver, *Ideas Have Consequences* (Chicago: University of Chicago Press, 1948), p. 10.

Contents

THE GOSPEL
according to
MADISON AVENUE

CHAPTER 1

Unstringing the Pilgrimage Racket

About once every Republican president, an advertisement crops up somewhere so splendidly phony that it could serve as the very ideal of quackery. Here is such an ad.[1] It begins by announcing in large type: "The perfect gift for female religious." If you have ever tried to pick out a present for a nun, you'll have wondered about that. Is it hankies? books? candy? statues? The perfect gift, the ad declares, is soap. Not just any soap, but Neutrogena. Under a drawing of a bar of this exciting soap comes the revelation, in capital letters: "IMPORTANT: NEUTROGENA IS ON THE APPROVED LIST."

Over the years since I first saw this ad I have talked to a considerable number of nuns and priests, and even to a bishop or two. Not one of them could tell me what the "approved list" was. Did the copywriter who dreamed up this ad really think Rome has an Index of Forbidden Toiletries? I can't find it in Denzinger-Bannwart, the handbook of definitions. The *Code of Canon Law* is no help. I looked into its index under "s" (for *sapo*); *sanguinis effusio* was followed by *satisfactio*. But no soap. Pliny used the word *sapo* to designate a pomade the Gauls plastered on their hair. Now *that*

[1] *Catholic Register,* National Edition, Dec. 11, 1955.

would not be approved for nuns—at least not in 1955, when the ad appeared. But Neutrogena is not hair pomade. It is—well, let me quote the ad:

> Indescribably gentle and mild, Neutrogena is the crowning achievement of a famed pharmaceutical chemist, Dr. Fromont of Brussels. It looks like soap but doesn't act like soap; for it is virtually [*quasi* as a theologian would say] a solidified cream made foamy and as neutral as pure water.
>
> Because it is on the Approved List, may we suggest Neutrogena as a gift for a Sister you wish to remember?

The laugh meter gives this ad an almost perfect rating. Logic is not so kind. The ad, in fact, is fraudulent. It is a perfect example of what I would describe as exploitative advertising, advertising that tries to capitalize on the deepest human emotions, like love of God and religion, love of country, fear, anger, and love of one's family. An ad which appeals to these emotions in selling its product is exploiting us. It is profoundly hypocritical. The Neutrogena spiel has tried to perpetrate a great hoax. Not on the nuns, of course, for they are intelligent women who have been buying soap all their lives without advice from the Congregation for Religious. It is a hoax on the layman, an effort to make him think that the Church has some sort of "Good-Housekeeping" seal of approval, that Neutrogena has been stamped by this seal, and that if we buy it we are somehow acting in conformity with the mind of the Church. *Sentire cum Ecclesia* at the notions counter, I suppose. One hopes that the hoax didn't come off. There is evidence it didn't. At least one Denverite phoned a vigorous complaint to the newspaper for running the ad. Lord knows how many others sighed and said nothing. (What extraordinary patience Catholics have!) The Neutrogena ad concludes:

> This rare soap from Belgium costs a dollar a cake—and is well worth it. At department stores and better cosmetic counters

everywhere; or send $1 to the address below and we'll be glad to serve you direct.

I'll bet they will. For $1 a cake, I'll serve you myself.

Another prime source of exploitative advertising is the pilgrimage racket. Is that too harsh a statement? Do pilgrimages constitute a racket, like the numbers? Some people think so (Hans Küng, for example). And with reason. Why? Because the ads which promote them are in fact selling a secular product (a vacation trip) by presenting it to us as a religious act (a pilgrimage). It is heartening to note that in a recent issue of *Sign* magazine (January, 1968), three such ads nowhere use the word "pilgrimage." One speaks of a "Catholic Alaska Tour." (You must guess which is Catholic, the tour or the state of Alaska.) Another announces a "Catholic Tour of the West," and a third is emblazoned with the terse message, "Jet Irish." A touch of chauvinism there, perhaps, since the tour spends but a few days in Dublin before hopping off to the Continent and the Holy Land. One senses that the Aer-Lingus Boeing will somehow be specially favored by the gods of the jet-stream, under the aegis of St. Patrick. No chance of being snakebit there.

So the pilgrimage has been transmogrified into the "Catholic tour." In what sense is such a tour Catholic? The majority of such trips do visit shrines and other places of importance to Christian history. But so do millions of non-Christian tourists, and even the jet set. But what about Alaska? What, indeed, about Yosemite Park and Yellowstone? Are there Catholic shrines there I have overlooked? I must write to Father Carl F. Clems about that "Catholic tour of the West." He is the spiritual director. Perhaps he can tell me how and why it is Catholic.

When I called such a tour a "secular product," I didn't mean that I despise it. People who work hard deserve a vacation, God knows, and if they want to visit Lourdes or

Fatima or Rome, what is wrong with that? Nothing, that I can see. But it isn't a Catholic tour, any more than a jaunt to Disneyland or Knott's Berry Farm is Catholic. It may be a way to recuperate from work (though that has been questioned), but it is not a pilgrimage, even though a "spiritual director" is riding along in the tour bus. His presence may make the tour less redolent of drunkenness and debauchery, but it doesn't make it Catholic, just as a plastic statue of the Sacred Heart stuck on your dashboard does not make your trip to the corner market a Catholic ride. The Catholic tour is, in fact, a vacation trip in company with a priest, who happens to be getting a free ride.

Each pilgrimage must have its spiritual director. That's part of the pitch. *Sign's* "Jet Irish" ad, for example, includes snapshots of four "distinguished" priests who will accompany each tour. They happen to be members of the same congregation that publishes the magazine. Each of them will get a free trip. The congregation, as a result, will escape the financial burden of sending them on a vacation somewhere else. That's how the racket operates. For a given number of tourists, the travel agency will provide a free trip for a priest. The whole operation is accomplished in a variety of ways. An individual priest can, on his own, drum up the necessary number of pilgrims and thus obtain his free ticket. Or a diocesan newspaper may advertise a pilgrimage under its own name and detail its editor or one of the priests of the diocese as spiritual director. And as we have seen, a religious order may promote free vacation trips for its members by advertising pilgrimages in the pages of its magazine. The latter two techniques are especially popular because the publications provide gobs of free advertising space. What the pilgrimages are all about then is this: free trips for the clergy and a bonanza for travel agencies, airlines, hotels, and sightseeing companies. I'm not against that. But when advertising promotes such activities as pilgrimages or Catholic tours, it becomes exploitative advertising, pure and simple. The pilgrimage has been turned into a racket.

And a very popular racket at that. So popular, in fact, that *Priest* magazine (April, 1968, p. 260) surrendered an entire page to the announcement of an extraordinary new "priest program" for "free Holy Land pilgrimages." Imagine that. Apparently such a crush of pilgrims engulfs travel agencies that *Priest* magazine must establish a kind of national directory or central governing board of spiritual directors, in order to coordinate their efforts to get free passes. What the program offers priests is "the opportunity of going to the Holy Land on a pilgrimage, without cost to you . . . departure on any Sunday of the year which you select." Any Sunday of the year yet! Perhaps this awesome development was necessitated by a last-minute rush to beat the travel tax President Johnson threatened to impose. I'm all for beating a tax, any tax, even to the extent of going on a "pilgrimage" to do it. But so long as advertising promotes such tours as Catholic, it is deceiving and exploiting us, stamping a secular pursuit with the seal of the Church and persuading countless good camera-toting American Catholics that their trip to Fatima or Paray-le-Monial or Glacier National Park is a yea-saying to Christ's call for penance. And it's high time somebody unmasked it, even if it costs him his free trip to Jerusalem.

The true nature of these so-called pilgrimages was never more candidly bared than by the editor of the *Advance Register,* Monsignor William Schaefers, Litt. M., J. Ll.D., in a series of articles that appeared in that paper in 1955. "This is the 21st in a series of articles on Catholic highlights in Europe." That's how the following "highlights" were introduced:

> You could see the Germans like their beer—this was plain.
> They like it, not in a mild and moderate way, but with their

whole hearts. However, they are not drunkards. They know how to drink. They may get to feeling happy (125 barrels of beer are consumed in one night at the Hofbrau), but they never grow vulgar, nor start fighting. We did not see one drunk in the Hofbrau. This added to our enjoyment of the evening we spent there. . . .

Every traveler to Munich visits the Hofbrau Haus, or simply —the Hofbrau. Established in 1589, it is the oldest and largest beer hall—or beer joint, if you will—in the world. It is owned by the city of Munich. Dinners are served only in the hall upstairs, which can accommodate a thousand customers. The hall on the ground floor is *the Hofbrau*. It is patronized by the common people and can accommodate 4,000 customers.

We spent an evening at the Hofbrau. We went there mainly to watch the Germans drink beer. First, however, we had dinner, with beer, in the hall upstairs. We all ordered Wienerschnitzel. It was a very satisfying *Abendessen*. As for the beer, well, German beer arouses enthusiasm. It is the best beer brewed anywhere. It is difficult to overstate its excellence.[2]

My teetotaling Protestant relatives down in Arkansas might readily agree that the Hofbrau, and its less splendid copies the world over, are indeed "Catholic shrines." And no one who has served with the military in Germany would contradict Monsignor Schaefers' enthusiastic remarks about the quality of beer brewed there. But somehow I find such delirious descriptions of beer-swilling anything but germane to what is supposedly a penitential trip to a sacred shrine. The *American College Dictionary* as a second definition of "pilgrimage" lists "any long journey." I wonder if that is not rather the first, and indeed the only, definition.

Other "products" than soap and trips are at times advertised in a pseudo-religious context. They are too numerous to itemize, but a recent advertisement in the *National Catholic Reporter* (June 5, 1968) can serve as illustration. The ad presents something new, " 'Celeste Rose' Grace

---

[2] *The Advance Register,* Feb., 1955.

Salt and Pepper Shakers." And then comes this reverential copy:

> Two beautiful reverent prayer "GRACE" shakers with gleaming gold like caps, each with full color "CELESTE ROSE" picture in lifelike cinemascope effect setting surrounded with a gold like embossed wreath. Elegance and beauty set a mood of thankfulness. They are practical and hold generous quantities of salt and pepper. A "GRACE BEFORE MEALS" and a "GRACE AFTER MEALS" prayer, imprinted in gold, adds drama. An ideal gift for any occasion.

Some enterprising ad man is trying to hoodwink the pious into buying salt and pepper shakers as an act of religion. If they fall for his bait, then the mood of thankfulness set by the shakers may grip the man who makes (and sells) the shakers, but not the man who rationally studies the advertisement. He will be horrified. I would go so far as to say: any time you read an ad which presents a secular item in a religious setting, you should automatically reject the appeal as fraudulent and shun the advertised product. If you don't, God knows what new ads might appear. I have my own premonitions in that regard and present herewith a couple of examples of what may come to pass.

> Buy the new Bountiful Bra. St. Andrew's Cross reverently stitched to each cup, in dainty monastery script, serving as a reminder to the wearer of the Source of all blessings. A beneficial warning to the trespasser of the gravity of the violation he may be contemplating. At more pious lingerie shops everywhere.

Or how about this:

> Try our all-new Rosary Snow Tires for those icy Lenten months. Rosary beads (actually, imported beans from the slopes of the Mount of Olives) are imbedded deep into the tread, in lieu of sawdust. As a result, the tires not only grip the roads but they beat a gentle tattoo of Ave Marias against the pavement as you drive. Next time someone asks you if you brought along your beads, tell him, "Yes, on all four wheels."

Exploitative advertising is not limited to the pages of the Catholic press, however. Anyone who has been exposed to the body of promotional literature emanating from the New York Stock Exchange has seen the exploitative approach in a most exalted form. Now, I'm not against the stock market or the buying of stock. I only wish I had a few thousand to invest. But when buying stock is presented as a patriotic deed, we are being hoodwinked. Buy stock and "invest in America," trumpets the Exchange. Who can resist an appeal like that? Can't you just picture your dollars leaping into some industry and strengthening it for the fight against the enemies of freedom? A truly stirring thought. And a false one. The money you invest goes to another investor and, in part, to the broker who gets his brokerage fee. His firm, of course, profits, as does the Exchange to which it belongs. But except for the case of an original issue of stock, the company under whose name the stock is sold gets nothing. Most of the stock transactions which are summed up daily by Dow-Jones are not "investments in America" except in the most general sense. And in that sense, waiting for the green light, zipping up your pants, having your brakes relined, and getting to work on time are equally investments in America.

So go ahead and buy stock, if you can afford to. You can reduce risk and obtain a dividend that, hopefully, will outpace the inflationary devaluing of our money. Those are selfish goals but not objectionable. Christ himself urged virtuous conduct by promising a reward. And your investments will put a healthy glow in the cheeks (and checks) of the Stock Exchange, which plays, it must be admitted, a vital role in our complex economy. But your purchase of stock is no more "an investment in America" than taking a Jet-Irish trip is a religious act or buying a cake of Neutrogena is thinking with the Church. And it's downright dishonest for ad men to tell us they are.

The word "advertising" as used in this book will at times denote even unpaid promotional literature, such as is ground out by public relations departments of universities and corporations. Such messages endeavor to sell a product or to create an image, and thus they deserve scrutiny. In terms of exploitative advertising, the richest lode to be mined is found in the campaign literature of various political parties and candidates and of the labor unions. It would require an entire book (or library of same) to analyze all the fraud to be discovered there. I shall look at but one appeal to be found in campaign advertising, the appeal based on fear. It is the most common. "Fear" is a kind of God-term to analysts of our nuclear age and has been defined as the source of everything from existential nausea to the hippie and yippie revolts. Political writers dote on it.

In 1952, for example, the Republican slogan was, "It's time for a change." And Ike won in a breeze after 20 years of Democratic sway. But the appeal is to fear, fear of political entrenchment with its connotations of pork barrel and corruption. Change in itself is no reason to vote one way or another, not unless it is change for the better. The 1952 slogan did not specify. A man who works in a kelp processing plant in San Diego gave me a copy of his union paper which appeared in 1964. In it a cartoon showed Barry Goldwater kicking the crutch out from under a crippled old lady. The appeal there is to fear, the fear of the aged for their security. Again in 1964, a televised Democratic pitch for our vote was made against the backdrop of a mushroom cloud. Fear. I think that the nadir of the exploitative pitch was made in the 1966 California gubernatorial race between incumbent Pat Brown and actor Ronald Reagan. Governor Brown was shown on the TV screen chatting with some Negro children. He asked one little girl, "Did you know it was an actor that killed President Lincoln?"

I wonder sometimes if it isn't futile to hope for an end
to base exploitation found in advertising like the above. I
keep remembering that Jesus said, "The poor you shall
have with you always." If he meant the poor in spirit, then
perhaps all we can do is hope they don't take jobs as
advertising copywriters or political hacks.

CHAPTER 2

Know Thy Product

The manufacturer of Regimen tablets and the advertising
agency that handled its $10 million account were indicted by
a Federal Grand Jury in Brooklyn in 1964 on a charge of
misrepresentation. The ad campaign that precipitated this
charge had pictured a number of individuals who, it was
claimed, lost weight dramatically by using the tablets. It
turned out that they were assisted by other devices, such
as a strict diet. The question was: did the Regimen tablets
cause the weight loss? The agency (Kastor, Hilton, Chesley,
Clifford and Atherton) through a spokesman replied to the
charge by accusing the government of trying to "create a
new and unheard of type of responsibility." And just what is
this "new and unheard of" responsibility the government
is trying to impose? Just the obligation of ad men to make
sure what they say about their product is true.

The editors of *America* remarked at the time: "This
would seem to imply that the agencies recognize no duty to
check on the claims of products they promote." [1] Whose
duty is it then? Surely not the consumer's. The Regimen
incident raises questions about the obligation of a writer,
any writer, to make his words correspond with the truth as

[1] *America*, Feb. 8, 1964, p. 181.

he sees it, an issue we can go into later. For now, let us formulate a commandment for ad men which will equip them to act responsibly and, incidentally, avoid the clutches of a grand jury. The commandment is: know thy product. The ad man who does not know his product is inviting disaster. Herewith a hilarious example.

In 1962, in an effort to obtain subscribers to a new magazine to be titled *The Bible Today,* the fathers at the Liturgical Press in Minnesota mailed out a prospectus which included, among other things, a reprint of an editorial by James M. Shea that had appeared in a Catholic newspaper. Here is how it went:

> All the explosive superlatives have been chewed to pieces and reduced to meaningless syllables by the motion picture industry and other language destroyers.
>
> As a result, when something that actually deserves superlatives makes its appearance, you have to fall back upon plain, simple English with which to recommend it.
>
> That is how it is with a new magazine which I haven't seen —which, in fact, hasn't been published yet. Its purpose is high, even noble. Its editorial staff is competent. The need for it is keen. And the price of it, relatively speaking, is low.
>
> With these things said, it occurs to me that we may be better off without the superlatives, after all.[2]

Poor Shea! How he despises those vile wielders of hyperbole who haunt the publicity dens in Hollywood. It isn't just that they exaggerate the virtues of their films. That would be bad enough. But they are destroying language as well. Quite a serious charge. And how does Shea counterbalance their meaningless, language-destroying blurbs? By promoting as a "praiseworthy project" (on which you and I should spend our money) a magazine he has never seen and which does not as yet exist. Heavens to Betsy! If that editorial is not an "explosive superlative" in

[2] "A Praiseworthy Project," *Denver Catholic Register,* June 28, 1962.

the profoundest sense of the phrase, I have never seen one. May I remind Shea, as a volunteer promoter of Biblical journals, and may I remind all advertising men of the great commandment: Know thy product. I am surprised that I have had to set that down. I had thought it was self-evident, like the principle of non-contradiction, or the infallibility in Washington, D.C., of John Maynard Keynes. Not so. It very much needs saying: Know thy product if thou wouldst know thy responsibilities. That is just what the Brooklyn grand jury was trying to say.

I mentioned above the writer's duty to write the truth as he sees it. That duty doesn't flow merely from laws against libel. It arises from the very nature of language. There is a very close connection between a writer and his words. Words are much like people, after all. They have a character (denotation) and a personality (connotation). They have an individual flavor and style. They often change their conduct when they change their company, just as people do. Small wonder that they are like us. In fact, they form a kind of projection of ourselves. They *are* us, as we reach out to touch others in the most meaningful way possible, by transmitting our beliefs, our hopes, our ideals— our very being. If, as Karl Jaspers says, thought is "indissolubly connected with the being of the thinker," [3] then the words in which that thought is given body are likewise a kind of verbal incarnation of the writer.

Philosophers from earliest times have made the Greek word *logos* (translated as "word" or "idea") a part of the common coinage of their thought. Heraclitus called God "the universal *logos*." Leucippus imagined that all reality happened *ek logou,* from the word. St. John thought the word *logos* worthy the honor of describing the Son of God: "In the beginning was the Word [*logos*], and the Word

[3] Karl Jaspers, *Reason and Existenz* (New York: The Noonday Press, 1955), p. 121.

was with God and the Word was God. . . . And the Word was made flesh." In my words I utter myself, I utter another me. Or to put it in a Johannine metaphor, my words are the flesh by which my thought is able to issue from me and dwell among men.

When a man sits down at his Underwood or IBM Executive and begins a novel, article, or copy for an advertisement, he had better realize that he is laying himself on the line. He is making a public confession, stripping himself naked to the popular gaze. In this sense writing is a kind of exhibitionism of the spirit by an egoist who thinks he has something to offer. (I plead guilty.) Perhaps the critic will better understand why writers are so sensitive to negative criticism: it is the writer himself who is being attacked, not just a congeries of disembodied words between the covers of a book. And perhaps, too, writers will better understand the philosophic crime they commit by writing lies, by deceiving, by exaggerating truth into a caricature—in short, by not knowing their product.

Of advertising that is downright fraudulent, little need be said. Dante thought that fraud is a vice peculiar to man and consigned its practitioners to a lower level in hell than archheretics (*Divine Comedy*, Canto 11). One would hope, all the same, that fraud is growing rare among advertisers. Of course it still exists, and occasionally even a Catholic newspaper unwittingly runs such an ad. In one instance (the diocesan paper shall remain nameless), a doll was advertised, with seven doll dresses, at the "bargain price of $2.98." A woman who answered the ad discovered to her dismay that the doll could have been purchased "downtown" for about 50 cents and that the dresses were only paper. Her view of the unimpeachability of the Catholic press was considerably soured by the incident. Post Office inspectors once brought to trial a man who had been selling for a few dollars "genuine engravings of George Washington." The engravings, you see, were three-cent stamps (remember them?).

Advertising, like life itself, is becoming more and more complex. A manufacturer is no longer content to have his brand name painted on a barn roof; instead his message must come to us, particularly on television, wrapped up in a cocoon of sensual explosives that go off in our minds with such force they block rational choice. The technique has been called a "high-input mix" and the result is what is known as "image advertising." A former chairman of the American Association of Advertising Agencies has defined it as the attempt "to reproduce a product experience before the product is bought." [4] Its aim is to sell us, not on the item's usefulness, but on its psychological value. And what is the result? Miles of film of handsome youngsters leaping, dancing, romping, splashing, grinning—in short, getting one helluva kick out of the advertised item just the way we will when we buy it. Tied into these frenetic scenes of apostolic enthusiasm over soda pop and detergents is an implicit scale of values. These values are the "ethical implications" of advertising and they are giving ad men and ethicians alike headaches. It is no longer enough to ask merely: does the ad claim that a product can do something which in fact it cannot do? Now the ethical implications must be put into a scale and weighed. For in their cumulative effect at least, they are presenting a particular way of life as an ideal. The gorgeous gals and guys in the hypnoworld of the commercial express in their delicious capers a set of values. We are being taught, when we watch them, that their value scale has validity, that we should buy it—and of course the product. The trouble is that the values ad men embody in their commercials are all geared to one aim: selling. Any value that would interfere with that goal must be

---

[4] "Honesty in Advertising," by Peter Bart, *Saturday Review*, Feb. 9, 1963, p. 62.

rigorously excluded. As a consequence, saints and ascetics, with their insidious doctrine of self-denial, are homeless, alien waifs on Madison Avenue. I imagine that if a copywriter should dig into the life of Francis of Assisi for ideas, it would only be in order to sell birdseed. All ad systems say, Go! Buy! If they don't create a need in us, they have failed. And that is the very reverse of asceticism, which aims at subjugating needs so that we may concentrate on what is central in life. Let the poor man of Assisi enjoy his exile from the world of advertising, that peripheral place of happy, indiscriminate buying, that grasshopperland of instant kicks, devoid of the fun-killing, malicious menace of tomorrow. He wouldn't be happy there anyway.

But what about us? We can't escape that world. Our magazines, newspapers, and TV screens are open windows into it, and we are inveterate peeping toms. At the very least, we can protect ourselves by urging advertisers to adopt some guidelines which will impart a taste of the Judaeo-Christian ethic to their ads. Ross A. Webber, assistant professor of industry at the Wharton School of Finance, University of Pennsylvania, has delved into this question of guidelines and formulated some rules which could assist the ad man to be responsible. They may be summarized as follows:

1. Advertising should not aggravate or pander to man's anxiety.

2. Advertising should not exploit man's instinct to conform, to keep up with the Joneses.

3. Advertising should not show contempt for human nature, e.g., by suggesting that this life is all there is.

4. Advertising should appeal to rational thought, not to emotion.[5]

That's a start. And other efforts are being made. Stockton

---

[5] "Advertising Responsibility," *The Catholic World*, Nov., 1966, pp. 87–91.

Helffrich of the National Association of Broadcasters, New York office, has drawn up a code to guide toy manufacturers in devising responsible advertising for toys. Comedian Johnny Carson's hilarious satires of toy commercials aptly illustrate the need for such a code. Sample: Don't glamorize the toy but "depict it, wherever possible, in a realistic play environment." We've come a long way from those portfolios of photographs the Skelly Oil Company used to give away to promote interest in Jimmy Allen and Speed Robertson. I guess it's progress.

The glamor ads, however, with their apocalypse of aseptic sex and carefree budgeting, form only one part of the world of advertising. There is another, nether world, familiar to readers of Catholic publications, and indeed of all publications in the limbo of low subscriptions. I mean the world of "original sin advertising." It is populated by those mean, one-column ads for worm remedies, acne cures, estrogenic cosmetics, hernia trusses, depilatories, skin-rash balms—all those products which so acutely remind us of our inherited moral taint. Let's face it. They are not highly regarded by a goodly portion of the intellectual community. The *New Yorker* has exiled them, along with women's undergarments, from its august pages. Even *Jubilee* has looked with pain on the large number of purgative ads appearing in Catholic magazines. I can understand *Jubilee's* embarrassment. After all, one wishes the Church press might command sufficient respect to entice a higher quality of advertising into its pages than those squibs for aperients and denture glue.

The gratitude of a small magazine when it obtains a glamor ad can take astonishing forms. In May, 1962, after the Chrysler Corporation had decided to buy advertising space in *Extension* magazine, the president of the Extension Society sent the following letter to priests all over the nation:

This letter and the attached brochure will introduce you to the 1962 PLYMOUTH and VALIANT automobiles of the CHRYSLER CORPORATION. The brochure gives the results of ten competitive tests conducted at Riverside, California. In these tests, a 1962 PLYMOUTH was pitted against comparable models of Ford and Chevrolet. As you will see, PLYMOUTH won eight out of the ten.

EXTENSION is carrying PLYMOUTH and VALIANT advertising on a regular basis and therefore the CHRYSLER CORPORATION becomes a supporter of the Catholic Church EXTENSION Society, the official Home Mission Organization of the Catholic Church in America.

We are anxious to cooperate with our advertisers in every way possible and if there is a new car or cars in your program in 1962 we will certainly be appreciative if you will TEST DRIVE a PLYMOUTH or a VALIANT before you buy.

Sincerely yours in Christ,
Rt. Rev. Msgr. J. B. Lux, S.T.D.

As a former working-reporter in the Catholic press, I can sympathize with Monsignor Lux in his eagerness to sell Plymouths and Valiants. Why should the secular press get all the gravy ads? On the other hand, why be ashamed of the original sin ads? I should think that an ad which reminds us of constipation or pimples reflects a more Christian view of human nature than the heaven-on-earth glamor advertising. The Catholic press runs such ads because, in most cases, they are all it can get and it needs the revenue. I see no great virtue in the *New Yorker's* spurning them, for it has other, more lucrative ones to take their place. Perhaps this supercilious disdain for laxative and corset ads is evidence of a renascence of the Pelagian heresy on the part of those who don't like to be reminded that they depend for their wherewithal on anybody, even God, or a girdle.

Advertising copywriters, if they are at all conscientious, may get bogged down hopelessly in that foggy bottomland of "ethical implications." The miasma arising therefrom clouds up even seemingly simple ads like those for milady's undergarments. "An innocent form of eroticism," the *Nation* dubs them from its lofty eminence.[6] Well, it may be so. Little is left in life that is simple, and why should advertising escape the curse of complexity? But whether ad men are selling utility or psychological value, whether they are disciples of a wonderful new audio-tactile cult or drudges worshiping the golden calf of hypnotic noise, one thing seems certain: the febrile intensity of their advertising is a reflection of the economic philosophy of men like Sumner Slichter. His credo is forthright: a good citizen will spend, not save, in order to feed our rapacious economy and keep it growing. There are no rainy days in this philosophy. So perhaps all the ad men are doing is helping you and me be good citizens. But I'm hanging on to my umbrella.

[6] *Nation,* June 22, 1963.

CHAPTER 3

For 'Discriminating' Headaches

The young seducer in Søren Kierkegaard's *Either/Or* makes a fascinating observation in his diary. "One never becomes giddy in a spiritual sense," he writes, "when one thinks only of a single thing." [1] I have a hunch ad men are familiar with this remark and have accepted it in its most literal sense. Their ads are seldom a "single thing." Just the reverse, in fact. They are stuffed with images and ideas so numerous they would make even the gloomy Dane himself giddy, giddy enough to buy. Let's apply a little Kierkegaard to a big modern drama.

Scene: the office in a corner of a large advertising agency somewhere East of Omaha. Seated at his desk munching tranquilizers is a frowning copywriter. He stares moodily at a small box lying before him. Wadded sheets of half-scribbled paper litter the floor.

Problem: he has to come up with an exciting new pitch for a dull old product. Well, the product isn't old, in name anyhow. It's another headache remedy. The ad man sighs and says to himself, "What can a guy do with acetylsalicylic acid that hasn't already been done?"

[1] Søren Kierkegaard, *A Kierkegaard Anthology* (New York: The Modern Library, 1946), p. 66.

Act I: in near despair he summons the agency's resident psychologist and unburdens himself.

"Gus," says the ad man, "I'm in a bind and need your help bad."

"What's the hang-up, Roger?"

Roger picks up the small box and hands it to Gus. "I need a pitch for this new headache remedy. Nothing I've tried seems to work."

Gus stares cryptically at the unlabeled box. "You need a name too?"

"Right. But that will depend on the pitch."

"I see. How about a young gal in a bikini slipping out of the water . . ."

"How about a young gal in the water slipping out of her bikini."

Gus does not appreciate the jest. "Slipping out of her water skis," he continues, "and reaching for one of these tablets. We could appeal to youth. And the outdoor setting would resonate in Westerners. They spend more on medicine than Easterners anyway."

"I tried that, but the boss didn't buy it. Said the young don't have headaches. And anyway, the client already has a remedy that sells big out West. He wants something specially tailored for the East Coast."

"Ah. That would mean a more rational appeal then?"

"Not necessarily. We could pitch the thing at the lower classes."

"You mean sell 'em what they don't need." Gus chuckles. "They went big for our cosmetics ads, remember?"

Roger smiles. "How about those tobacco harvesting machines we sold the poor Southern farmers. I'm still picking up checks for that coup."

"Of course," Gus remarks, "there's a danger if we tie the product too closely to the low mobiles. They're only a quarter of the market, or less."

"You're right, Gus. I'd like a big sales response to show later to the client on a chart. He'd think the ad did it."

"I don't suppose these pills actually have anything new to offer the customer. I mean, like they don't work faster, do they?"

"I'm afraid they don't. And anyway, we don't want to get mixed up in that speed race. The people must be sick of it by now."

"Given a different Gestalt, it might work. Well, let me chew on it a while, will you Roger?"

"Don't take too long. The big man's bugging me something fierce."

Act II: same office, same *dramatis personae*. Psychologist Gus enters beaming. Though he speaks casually, a note of triumph is not lacking.

"I've got it, Roger. Your new campaign is all ready to go."

"You consulted your tea leaves?"

"I'll ignore the innuendo and let my ideas speak for themselves."

"What deep and hidden motive are we going to appeal to?"

"Listen to this, Roger. Every man has a deep-seated need to be loved, to be respected, to feel that other people think highly of him."

"So what's the pitch?"

"We'll appeal to their vanity."

Roger shrugs. "It's been done."

"Ah yes, but not like this. I'm taking a new slant."

"New?"

"New. The angle is the headache."

"How's that? You mean there's more'n one kind of head-ache? I've heard of the migraine. . . ."

"No," Gus interrupts, "this isn't that trite scientific appeal. The kinds of headaches I'm talking about are those that ordinary bums have and those that geniuses and leaders have."

"There's a difference?"

"We'll make people think there is."

"Ah," murmurs Roger, as the dawn begins to break.

"If you had a choice of headaches, would you rather have Einstein's or some ordinary jerk's? We'll pitch our new headache pills to the bright boys."

"But there aren't enough of us," says Roger.

Gus frowns. "You don't get it. The point is, everybody thinks he's bright. At least he wants other people to think he is. When he buys our new pills, he's telling the world, and the drugstore clerk, that he's one of the high I.Q. set, a successful man, an innovator."

"I get it. And no one will want to buy Aspirin or Bufferin or Excedrin after this because it would look like an admission of ignorance, like they're confessing they're morons or boobs."

"Exactly. If a man asks for Aspirin now, the clerk will think he's a high school drop-out—or we'll make the customer think that's what the clerk will think."

"It's brilliant!"

"Psychology has certain insights."

"What are we going to call the stuff?"

"What do you think of Hi I.Q. Headache Remedy? Or Hi I.Q. for short? For discriminating headaches."

"Terrific, Gus. But maybe we could shorten it. It's a small box. How about just Hi Q. I wonder if there's some harmless drug beginning with the letter "q" that we could toss into it and advertise as being the big difference between this product and what's already on the market?"

"You'd best talk to the chemists about that. It's not my bag." Gus exits, humming the immortal opening bars of Beethoven's Fifth Symphony. Roger begins to scribble on a notepad, talking out loud as he does so.

"Hi Q for the discriminating headache. The poet slaving at his canto. The artist at his atelier. The scientist at his computer. The executive in command of men. Leaders like these have big and important headaches, not the ordinary and common sort. Just ask a member of Mensa. He'll know what we mean. You bright guys, use Hi Q. The rest of you, eat your hearts out."

Grinning, he snatches up his copy and heads for the boss's office, singing a little ditty as he goes. The lyrics are:

> For High I. Q.'s
> Who'd lose the blues
> Our headache pills
> Are today's big news.

The curtain falls.

At least, the curtain almost falls, because an ad very similar to this has actually been presented on the television screen lately. I can't report just what success it had in exploiting our need to be thought highly of. The awful point is, just such a pitch was really made. Depressing, isn't it? Such a pitch isn't a single thing. It's a complex commercial, making use of one of the "discoveries" of Gestalt psychology which shows that we don't respond to the individual stimulus but rather to the item (the headache pills in this instance) in relation to everything that surrounds it in the ad. We respond not just to the pills but to the whole kaleidoscope of images in which they are pitched at us. Of course, the ad man is attempting to make us believe in his product. If our belief is compelling enough, we will probably buy it. In the case of the headache pills, if our belief in them is particularly strong, they will cure our headache in most cases, a fact not unknown to witch doctors, or to the other kind.

When we look at an ad, according to Gestalt thinking, we react to the total situation. In a soap commercial, we don't respond simply to the soap but also to the glamorous starlets or models bathing in its suds, to the scientific men in white coats singing its praises, to the young men rubbing it over their musculature, to the confident sound of the announcer's voice, to the quality of the music (if any) that accompanies the message, as well as to a lot of other factors that even psychologists aren't wise to yet. The result is an ad whose message is based on innuendo. The ad men want us to think that their product will do something which in fact it cannot do. If they make that claim outright, we would laugh them out of the marketplace. Instead, they suggest the claim, they make us think it is true. If a soap company claimed that scrubbing our faces with their soap would make us beautiful as movie queens, or if a cigarette manufacturer declared that smoking his product would increase male virility, no one would believe it. Their ads, therefore, imply or suggest these results. It's innuendo.

Most snob appeal advertising is based on innuendo. I hesitate to use the word "snob" because it is so popular with the egalitarians who claim that no one is better than anyone else. Originally a snob was a shoemaker's apprentice, then a common man. More recently a snob was someone who sucked up to the rich and famous or who thought himself better than other people. I shall use "snob" anyhow, because it is expressive and to the point, but I want to make a preliminary remark. It is one thing for us to be provoked at a man because he thinks he is better than we are. It is quite another thing to deny that he is, or can be, better. Maybe he is. Let's face it. A lot of people are smarter, more industrious, handsomer, and more gifted than we are. Calling them "snobs" won't alter the fact.

Human nature, to judge from the evidence, does manifest a funny kink that makes us like to rub shoulders with the "great." Fans of movie stars show this kink in a cruder form. Name-droppers are guilty of a variation of it, a kind of vicarious shoulder-rubbing, done while the great are *in absentia.* It is safer and highly recommended to anyone who is fearful of rejection. Trying to get on the dais with the noted speaker, shoving into a photograph being made of the "top brass," and leaping onto the football field to walk among the padded mesomorphs—all these are innocent enough forms of this compulsion to mingle with the mighty, to eat high off the psychological hog. Since for most of us it is difficult or impossible to be physically among the famous, we achieve the same feeling by showing that our tastes are the same as theirs. This is where advertising comes into the picture.

"Old World Charm Invades Lake Tahoe," murmurs the ad in the *Wall Street Journal* (April 22, 1968), announcing Tyrolian Village at North Lake Tahoe. If you look behind the disguise, you'll see that this ad is appealing to our vanity. But a popular myth (or unstated premise) is hiding in the underbrush. If it's imported, so the myth runs, it's better. We've all encountered this myth in the scripture of the ad men. A lot of people believe it too. It has handicapped domestic cheese producers, woolen manufacturers, and vintners. At one time, I am told, the popular crush on imported goods was so passionate that some domestic manufacturers actually shipped their goods outside the continental limits before putting them on the market just so they could legally label them as "imported." If it's imported, it's superior: thus the snob ad. Perhaps the concept "old world" does suggest to some folks a degree of sophistication, *savoir faire,* and quality that the home-grown item seems to lack. By buying the imported item, they show that they share in those urbane and suprasensitive virtues of the continent. Sports car buffs who dismiss all American automobiles as "Detroit junk" are usually victims of this snobbish idolatry of the imported. So are women who don't care what frock or perfume they wear, as long as it's French.

A logician would call the logical fallacy of such advertising "a specious type of enthymeme." Don't let that statement frighten you off. After all, "gallinaceous fowls are oviparous" means only that hens lay eggs. An enthymeme is simply an argument in which something is left unsaid. But if what is unsaid is false, the conclusion is untrue. When an advertisement encourages us to buy because the item is imported, it is inferring (but not explicitly saying) that being imported means superiority. But that may not be true. Or suppose an ad agency develops a new campaign for a girdle maker. After a few months, sales of that particular make of girdle begin to rise. The agency tells the client: our ad campaign is a success. Maybe not. Just because the rise in sales came after the new ad campaign, one cannot conclude that it came because of the campaign. There is not always an empirical way of proving that ads spur sales. Perhaps something else boosted girdle sales, like a new style of women's clothing that demands greater constriction of the female figure. This latter fallacy is called the "post hoc, ergo propter hoc" fallacy, and frequently victimizes managers of major league baseball teams. If losses follow their accession as manager, they are reasoned to be causes of the losses and are fired. Management wants the public to think it is doing something.

When Bob Richards assures us he has eaten Wheaties all his life and when Paul Hornung rhapsodizes over Chevrolets or Jantzen swim trunks, we are in the presence of another enthymeme called "the argument from authority." It is often a specious or false form of reasoning because in many cases the so-called authority knows nothing about the product he is lauding, but is excited mostly about the size of the residuals his endorsement will win. I shall never forget a professor of philosophy who remarked one day in class, "The argument from authority is the weakest form of argument." A student asked, "How do you know?" And the professor replied, "Because St. Thomas said so." Well, Dave Bing likes Buicks and Buddy Hackett recommends a particular brand of potato chip. What are we to conclude? Not (if we would be logical) that a Buick or specific brand of chip is worth buying. It may be, but not because a basketball star and comedian say so. When Monsignor X is advertised as the purchaser of a new electric organ, we are being assaulted by the argument from authority. If the monsignor bought the organ (and he's the vicar general), then it must be good. Not so. I am happy to report that as people become more intelligent and better educated, they grow less susceptible to this form of reasoning. Since the argument from authority is not on the wane, what are we to conclude?

Advertisers, like most of the rest of us, have a mad fondness for the word "new." Some deep-rooted part of our nature squirms sweetly to newness. We are reassured, I guess, by this perpetual resurrection of things all round us. A new knit suit, new textbook, new car, new coat of paint— are they not in a sense pledges of some kind of immortality? By the laws of entropy, the whole universe is unwinding, spending its quota of energy, exhausting itself. The thought of oceans of galaxies strewn like bleak, dead embers across a burnt-out space is not a prepossessing one, even if it won't occur for an eon or two. And in particular, our personal plunge toward old age and death is a bit discomfiting. New things seem to guarantee stability, permanence, perpetual youth.

On a more practical level, we are likely to think that what is new is better, a legacy of the Whig theory of history which held that life was an uninterrupted succession of advances from lower to higher plateaus of achievement. The ad man, borrowing from the Whigs, announces that his detergent is new. The implication is: it is therefore better.

This is called the argument from modernity (another form of enthymeme that may well be fraudulent). Although the resourcefulness of scientists has scarcely been tapped, one wonders just what further improvements can be made, for instance, to soap. It cleans, it smells good, it leaves the skin intact over the bones. Perhaps in future it may make us glow in the dark or render our derma impervious to deadly gamma rays. In any case, logic reminds us that what is new may not be better. It may, in fact, be worse.

Our experience in several World Wars has seriously exaggerated this psychological mania for what is new, what is to come. The lookingforwardness we nurture was given a lethal boost in the military camps, where men cosseted their nettled egos by continually reminding themselves, "It'll be different, better, at the next post." My own companions in ground school thought constantly of the day they would begin to fly. But in primary training, they were looking forward to basic. And at basic training they spoke only of operational training. And so on.

A fellow collegian, veteran of World War II, often asked me to his home for dinner. "There's a terrific TV program I want you to see with us," was the way his invitation usually went. We would rush through dinner, with no comment being made on its excellence but only on the great show coming up on television. At last the show would begin. It might have been a crime thriller, who knows? But my friend would watch with ill disguised disinterest. He had already begun to look forward (posterior vision, it can be called). "There's a really great movie on next week," he would remark. "You'll love it. It's called *The Night of the Blood Beast*. Hope you can drop by." And so on.

What is going on in such a mentality is a neurotic intensification of natural (not supernatural) hope. It is based on a tragic failure to appreciate, to prize, the present moment, which if you think about it is all we've got. We are not fully living each moment. *Now* has become a hurdle we must leap over to get to *then*. Thus, education is looked on simply as an obstacle to a degree. Not a unique and enriching experience in itself, but something to be gone through, got by, endured, in anticipation of commencement, which in turn will be gotten through stoically in anticipation of that "big job." And so on.

The poet Bécquer has beautifully touched on this quirky posteriority of our vision:

> *La gloria y el amor tras que corremos,*
> *Sombras de un sueño son que persiguimos.*
> *Despertar es morir.*

And that means roughly: "The love and glory we run after are only dreams we have while asleep. To die is to wake up." We make prodigal outlay of the little time at our disposal, squandering it at a hectic pace, without being fully conscious of the present moment. Our eyes are so riveted on the posterior (that means "future" in Latin, not backside) that we forget the present. We are asleep to it.

But God, who knows us better than we think, will put an end to this somnolent stage of being, of existence. When we die, we will hopefully enter that state of being in which there is only the eternal *nunc,* the nowness of God. There will be no past, except as a reminder of God's mercy and wisdom. There will be no future, nor any need for one. We will have perfectly achieved everything good our nature is capable of being and knowing and doing. There will be no "and so on's."

The reverse form of enthymeme from the argument from modernity is called the argument from antiquity. Or: if it's old, it's better. It appeals to the old folks. Lately, devotees of the rosary have been struggling to refurbish its badly tarnished image by urging us to pray "the medieval rosary." I'm not certain just how the medieval differs from the modern rosary, but the fact is that being medieval does not make it an improvement. If you come across a biscuit advertisement that tells you they "are like grandma used to make," before you buy I suggest you ask, "Whose grandma?" When the commercial for Gold Medal Flour announces, "Mothers have been baking memories with Gold Medal for four generations," you know that some copywriter is making a desperate appeal to your nostalgic reverence for "the good old days," and the good old biscuits too.

The argument from antiquity has adulterated other, broader forms of advertising. I mean the writings of some philosophers and theologians who have a message to make, a product to sell. I can't help but feel Yves Simon was guilty of antiquarianism when he began a lecture in Denver, Colorado, in 1952 by stating, "I do not hesitate to say that the school of St. Thomas is the only school with anything of value to say on free will. The word of truth is found only in St. Thomas." [1] Equally guilty of antiquarianism are those musical purists who insist that in the performance of Handel's *Messiah* there be no more than 20 singers and no trombones at all. That, they note, is the way Handel himself arranged the first performance. But the purists are ignorant of the fact that Handel could only get 20 singers for that first performance; moreover, no trombones were available to him in Dublin at the time.

Liturgists are guilty of antiquarianism when they demand that the Church return to some ancient form of the liturgy, e.g., that of Hippolytus, as to an ideal. So are those Christians who accuse their ministers of heresy for not interpreting the Scriptures exactly as their grandfathers did. New translations of the Bible are at times rejected

[1] The quotation is from a personal transcript made at the time the lecture was delivered.

solely because they are different from an older, more familiar version. A fine old gentleman of my acquaintance, when I asked why he refused to read the Revised Standard Version, replied, "If the King James version was good enough for Jesus, it's good enough for me."

Philip Evergood's painting *My Forebears Were Pioneers* shows a grand dame seated regally in her stiff-backed chair before a crumbling rococo house. I am always reminded of the antiquarians when I look at that painting. They, like Evergood's matriarch, appear to be looking wistfully backwards to past triumphs and ancient glories, while the present threatens to topple into ruins for want of strong arms and hard backs and sound minds—and indeed for want of logical thinking.

"Imported 'Leopard Robe,' " says the ad in the *Ladies' Home Journal* (April, 1968). "Leopard robe" is in single quotes because it is imitation. *San Diego* magazine for June, 1967, features an ad for an interior decorator in Rancho Santa Fe that reads: "The charm of a European shop in a country village setting." Is it that aliens are more adept than we at making ersatz leopard skin? Do European shops have all that charm? But what is more vital, do I find myself vibrating harmoniously to the message implicit in such advertising? If I do, then I need to study the specious forms of enthymeme listed above. And I also need to be reminded that my value depends in no wise on my being associated with the company or with the tastes of the great and famous. A book that professes to deal with advertising, even advertising in the widest sense of the term, should not dip into the subject of what makes a man valuable. Whatever it is (self-fulfillment, union with God, freedom from hang-ups, unselfish service to the community), it has nothing to do with the priggish vainglory that the snob ads appeal to. If people are going to value me, it will be for other reasons than that I have a dozen imported cashmere sweaters, a cellarful of French champagne, a summer house that looks like a Swiss chalet, or a copy of the book "everybody's" reading.

Like everything else in life, advertising is going to change and develop. It will react to such restructurings of our society as that effected by the change in the average age. The under-25 age group, which is rapidly approaching majority status, is said to spend about $20 billion a year. Advertising will reflect that buying power. I don't mean to imply that the increase in the number of young buyers is the cause of stupidities in advertising. (That might be an example of the *post hoc, ergo propter hoc* fallacy.) But it is a fact that young people are peculiarly susceptible to certain logical fallacies contained in ads. Youth are gregarious, apt to ape one another, and not as likely, I think, to make mature emotional responses to what they read. Having said that much, I may as well admit that I am "over 30." But we old-timers need a pepper-upper these days, some reminder that we are not quite as ridiculous, hypocritical, and stagnant as some of the youngsters maintain. Let us vindicate our senile selves, at least to this extent: we can have a good laugh at the snob ads as pure commercial nonsense aimed at the vanity and painful imitativeness of the young. And then we can act accordingly. We can buy with our heads.

Nothing would so quickly shut off the drip-drip-drip of quack ads as a vigorous resistance to them on the part of the public. As Earl Kintner put it, when he was chairman of the Federal Trade Commission: "In the blunt language of the street, the gyp seller depends on the sucker buyer and can't exist without him." [2] If we can't convert the gyps, then we must educate the suckers, ourselves. Apparently we haven't been doing that job.

[2] Cited in *Time,* Jan. 4, 1960.

I have no intention at this time of adding my name to that considerable list of critics who have panned American education. Yet the existence of specious advertising in some quantity would seem to argue that our schools have not convincingly won their war against ignorance. Illiteracy may be at its nadir, and a college degree, for better or worse, is rapidly becoming Requirement A for the most menial job in business. So how can it be that education has failed? Today we are sending unprecedented numbers of our youth to school, yea, even to colleges and universities. Yet spurious advertising exists and, worse, succeeds. How can it be?

History provides uneasy answers to that question. The most notable "advertising" triumphs of modern times were scored by the Nazi and Communist ideologies, which managed to sell vast numbers of people on political and economic creeds which deny basic human rights and pretend to advance human dignity while committing the foulest crimes against humanity. How was such a thing possible? How, when illiteracy was at its lowest ebb, could huge masses of people swallow vicious propaganda to such an incredible extent? Had it happened in the Middle Ages, we could comfortably blame it on the Church. The ignorance and naiveté of the "Dark Ages" fairly jumps out at anyone who studies, for instance, the legends of the saints. What can we say of a culture that accepted as factual the "life" of St. Rumwold, an infant who died at the age of three days but not until he had made an eloquent profession of faith to all in his presence and even preached a long sermon to his parents? Yet more wonderful by far is the naiveté of a culture that can accept belief in a super race or in a classless society. What accounts for it? Not illiteracy. In fact, it was precisely literacy itself that helped assure the success of Nazism and Communism, just as it is the high literacy rate in America that assures quack advertisers of a vast and gullible audience.

That statement deserves some explanation. I am trying to say that literacy, without education, does no more than expose a man to a horrendous onslaught of words, words that crash upon him from every direction, pitching him about achingly in their emotional tempest, deafening him, half-drowning him in verbal spindrift. As a result he becomes either a believer in whatever it was he read last, or more likely he stops reading and listening and devotes himself to hobbies and recreation or to TV game shows—to anything but the strepitous rigors of thought. I am not suggesting that illiteracy is the answer to shoddy advertising. But neither is literacy. The answer is education.

I guess I am talking, in part anyway, to educators, and I hope I will be forgiven my audacity. The credentials I bring to the task are slim, but the climate is right for it. Just the other day an oceanographer, wise in the ways of dredge hauls, expounded on the intricacies of speculative theology. And I note that John Galbraith in *The New Industrial State* (p. 352) hands down some olympian judgments on architecture. What I have to say about education has been said before: we must teach the young, not simply subjects, but rather the tools of learning, chief of which, as I see it, is logic. To a graduate of a Jesuit college (as I am), mention of logic will evoke harrowing memories of all-night wrestling matches with epichiremes, sorites, enthymemes, polysyllogisms, and kindred mysteries. That is fine for the university, but, as Sidney Hook has pointed out, what is needed is something on the primary level, a simpler approach that

plunges the student into an analysis of language material around him. By constant use of concrete illustrations drawn from all fields, but especially from the fields of politics and social study, insight is developed into the logical principles of definition, the structure of analogies, dilemmas, types of fallacies and the reasons *why* they are fallacies, the criteria of good hypotheses, and related topics.[3]

Education is, in a sense, the training of our ability to see the connections between things. Logic will tell us if the connections men draw between one thing and another are reasonable and flow from the evidence at hand. I should like to add, as a source of logical fallacies, the field of advertising, and that for two reasons. First, children are exposed to so much advertising, especially on television, that it would be criminal not to let them in on its comical non sequiturs. Second, in few other fields are so many unusual and, indeed, illogical, relationships drawn. A grade school geography class, for instance, might fruitfully explore the causal relationship (if any exists) between mountainous terrain and coffee flavor, with apologies to Folger's. Students in the social sciences might be interested to know if eating Carnation Instant Breakfast really cures those getting-up-in-the-morning blues. Peter Pan, playing a twentieth century tune for the kiddies, assures them that its peanut butter has a "husky, grown-up taste." I have lately read of a 3-year-old girl who began to menstruate because of eating her grandmother's face cream which was rich in hormones. But the nexus between peanut butter, even Peter Pan's, and adulthood is less clear. Perhaps the copywriter in this case, observing the children's lemming-like stampede to their majority, feared that they were about to spurn peanut butter, along with toys and dolls, as so much infantile impedimenta.

The man who is merely literate is the victim of words; the truly educated man is their master. Widespread literacy has made mass communications feasible; education will

---

[3] Sidney Hook, *Education for Modern Man* (New York: Alfred A. Knopf, 1963), pp. 147–148.

render them responsible. The technology of transmitting words and ideas has outstripped progress in education, it would seem, and it is possible that this gap, not that between the generations, is responsible for much of the turmoil of our times. When we are daily fed enormous quantities of data, it becomes more imperative that we develop our ability to evaluate and interpret them.

One rather simple recommendation that logic makes in regard to advertising is that we spend more time analyzing the product itself and less (or no) time studying the ads. Many people are doing just that, as is witnessed by the growth of consumers' research magazines which give independent and objective reports on all sorts of products from automatic transmissions to frozen foods. These magazines are the fruit of skepticism, an altogether healthy sort of skepticism in my judgment, which should serve as a grim warning to ad men of what can happen if masses of people lose faith in commercials and begin to disbelieve them altogether.

Education, with its proper accent on logic, will help those on both sides of the ad, consumer and copywriter alike, by rooting in them a firm and uncompromising fidelity to truth and to the processes by which we arrive at it. Our obligation to educate ourselves is more pressing today than ever. It is a lifelong task, one we must busy ourselves at, even if need be in the classroom, and even at the risk of emerging with some talismanic letters (B.A., Ph.D.) stuck to our academic backsides like a prehensile tail. But not just any education will do, and certainly not one that parades man through history as a lucky, if hairy, ape who happens to rut year round, or as a complex bundle of molecular particles looking for redemption in the final combustion of a chrome-plated crematorium. Education is valueless if it fails to recognize who man is, why he is here, and where he is going. In short, "Education is of no earthly use unless it begins from God and leads back to him." [4]

And now that I think of it, the same thing can be said of advertising.

[4] F.H. Drinkwater, *Educational Essays* (London: Burns Oates, 1951), p. 3.

CHAPTER 4

You Can't Change the World

"This record . . . The Living Rosary . . . can change your life."

That's what the ad says, offering *metanoia* at 33 r.p.m. Whenever an advertisement promises drastic changes, whether in the whiteness of your kitchen sink or in the whiteness of your immortal soul, it reminds me of a press conference held a few years ago in Denver. Father James Keller, founder of the Christophers, was to be a featured speaker. A Regis College student, James B. Denigan, at a meeting prior to the conference, made what I always considered an erudite suggestion. He proposed that the conference motto be revised from "You Can Change the World" to "You Can Better Inform the World." His argument, I recollect, was that no one, least of all a journalist, can change anybody but himself. Although he was overruled in an eponymous deference to Father Keller, his reasoning stands and can be used against the Living Rosary ad. The record can change no one. It can inform or, perhaps, inspire. But that's all. To expect more of it is to be a sucker.

What is the source of such "promised land" advertising as this Living Rosary pitch? It springs, I think, from that cardinal virtue of every organization man, enthusiasm, or pitching-in-ness. Enthusiasm, no doubt, generates hard work, loyalty, selfless dedication to the cause that refreshes—and, in the bargain, grievous moral and intellectual aberrations if it goes undisciplined. Monsignor Knox gave enthusiasm an entire book and us a candid look at the messes it has made in various corners of Christendom. The Quietist controversy, according to no less an authority than Pierre Pourrat, owes its genesis to Fenelon's "ardent temperament" [1] (that's French for enthusiasm). A fanatic is nothing if not enthusiastic, be he a Klansman wrapped in a sheet or a professor wrapped in an idea.

The advertising man, as we should expect, is enthusiastic about his product. At least his copy reads that way. It has to. Who would buy a pair of shoes on the strength of a half-hearted (or half-souled) advertisement? Ads are supposed to get us excited about buying, to show us what we are missing, to give us a toothsome little foretaste of the joys of owning the product. A psychologist at Creighton University once pointed out to me the curious similarity between beatnik poetry and the mystic elucubrations of St. John of the Cross. He has something there. But there is, as well, a kinship between St. John's verbal reconstructions of mystical experience and the prose of ad men. The ad is related to our buying the product as John's poetry is related to the beatific vision. The rhetoric of both shares the quality of unintelligibility and obscurity. The reason is that the ad man, like John, lives and has his being in a mystique of enthusiasm. His beatific vision is the sight of millions buying his product, a development which naturally makes him itch with excitement and accounts for the exaggeration and excessive promises that flood his copy. His addiction to hyperbole leads to delicious little ironies. What are we to think when four different cigarettes are

[1] Pierre Pourrat, *Christian Spirituality* (Westminster, Md.: Newman Press, 1955), Vol. IV, p. 205.

lowest in tars? When four different headache remedies all work fastest?

"It isn't fair," the ad man may reply, "to subject my copy to linguistic analysis." St. John of the Cross felt the same way, sharing the ad writer's reluctance to have his copy rigidly analyzed. In 1584 he wrote: ". . . it would be ignorance to think that sayings of love understood mystically . . . can be fairly explained by words of any kind." [2] Fair or not, analysis is necessary since the ad man, no less than the Carmelite, is trying to teach us a way to think and to act. We had better be sure of the exact nature of his message before we accept or reject it.

Hopefully most of us see through the superlatives swaddling the message and make out, if dimly, the tiny body of truth underneath. I say "hopefully" because if hyperbole didn't work, ad men would stop using it. So someone is being conned by all this yelling over best and quickest and tastiest. Not you and me, but someone. Enthusiasm has begot exaggeration, and for the time being we must live with it. It is everywhere: in the political gesture (assassinations and ritual self-immolations), the motorist's comic-book response to highway discourtesy, fashion manias, youth's rebellion against the hardships of reality. Exaggeration, it would seem, is the modus operandi of modern man. Why should advertisers be immune from it? Not that they have cornered the market on provocational gobbledygook. A case might be made that their prose is considerably less flawed than that of, say, sociologists.

But their prose is often not honest. The Living Rosary ad is not honest. Is it a question of semantics? But lying is often a question of semantics. The "change in life" promised by the Rosary ad is, as the Greek word *metanoia* makes clear, a self-readjustment that goes to the roots of one's

[2] St. John of the Cross, *Spiritual Canticle* (Garden City: Doubleday, 1961), pp. 40, 41.

being and involves a radical change in one's outlook. "Turning over a new leaf" is far too shallow a metaphor to describe this change. Uprooting old habits and planting new ones is more like it. That means practice, exercise, time. Even so celebrated a guru as Maharishi Mahesh, tutor of Beatles and other forms of life, was sharply criticized for teaching "instant yoga." Just grab a foam-rubber cushion, he said in effect, and when the yen is upon you, meditate. Just like that. Not so, replied his critics in New Delhi. "This man can't sell yoga as if it were instant coffee." Nor can the Living Rosary record change my life. Enthusiasm makes the ad man say that it can, to exaggerate its capabilities, even to say at times that we cannot live without it. The truth is we need precious little in this life in order to be happy, but I suspect that is too austere a dogma for the advertising industry or the regnant school of economics to accept.

While they are hesitating, let me remind them of what happened to the Church for permitting over-enthusiastic ad men to get away with murder in preparing their copy. One would think that ecclesiastical writers could find plenty in the Church that deserves superlatives. Yet what did they light on in the past as worthy of adulation? Relics and indulgences! Dear Lord, what reams of hapless parchment were larded with orgiastic praise of relics and indulgences. And what is left of all this paper? Bare ruined quires, that's what, and the late birds who sang thereon were anything but sweet. Enthusiastic is what they were. Wrong is what they were.

Imagine this historical scene, recorded by the pagan writer Jamblichus: Christians of the Eastern Church busy as discount butchers chopping the bodies of the saints into a jillion tiny cutlets so that there would be relics enough to go around. Such slaughter-house antics were the product of too much enthusiasm over relics. And as for indulgences, whatever merit they possess was pretty well eliminated from popular consideration by the pious exaggerators who goaded Luther into such a frenzy. The faithful were tricked into thinking that they couldn't get along without relics and indulgences, and thus they grew ga-ga over the sight of some saint's pubic hair, or a feather from the Archangel Gabriel, or (would you believe it!) the genuine prepuce of our Lord. In more recent times the Gideon Society, with its lust for planting copies of the Bible all over hotel and moteldom, is guilty of a like exaggeration. It seems to credit the mere act of reading Scripture with a kind of magical power. A perusal of the Bible provides far more benefits than, say, a reading of *Playboy,* and both relics and indulgences definitely have their place in the spiritual scheme of things. But all three are in danger of being exiled from the modern mentality (if indeed they have not already been) because churchly publicity writers promised too much from them.

Would to God that pious hyperbole were a thing of the past. Unfortunately it is not. Pastors are familiar with a periodical titled *Candle Light,* which is published "as a help to Catholic pastors in preparing publications and bulletins, and as a service to editors of Catholic newspapers and magazines." A typical issue leads off with a poem by Lenore Wheeler Fleming called "Before the Blessed Sacrament." The fifth line reads as follows: "This is our best. Our best! These lighted candles . . ."[3] In her defense, it must be said that Lenore goes on to make a little list (one hopes it isn't taxative) of some items that are "our best." She includes burning incense, hymns, prayers, the monstrance, snowy linens—and oh yes, the Eucharist. Primacy of place, you will note, goes to candles. Shades of disgusted Jamblichus, watching fervent relic-seekers hack up the bodies of the saints!

Candle Light, I note, is sponsored by seven candle manufacturers, listed atop the masthead, so that we can know the

[3] *Candle Light,* No. 67, Sept.-Oct., 1960.

source of all this enthusiasm over candles. And in case you should care to pursue the subject further, the address of the Candlelight Guild is (or was) 19 W. 44th Street, New York 36. The purpose of the guild is "to distribute informative articles to the Catholic press on the traditions, religious significance, and liturgical uses of candles and votive lights." Among the supporters of the guild are the same seven candle makers. I shouldn't wonder. My own grave misgivings about the value of candles were not dispelled by the information, cited on page 2, that in the eighth century there were "no less than 1,365 candles" in St. Peter's in Rome.

I can hear the candle makers now exclaiming, "Come off it! Candles have always been a part of Church ritual. You yourself are guilty of exaggeration." If I am, then how does one explain the millions of the faithful who year after year spend their dollars on vigil lights until the very Catholic air reeks of beeswax? Better of that, I suppose, than of cigarettes or beer. But if you take your theology from Vincent de Paul instead of Will & Baumer, you will prefer that the money have gone to the 700,000 dwellers in the *favelas* of Rio de Janeiro, or to the braceros, or to our own American poor—or, God knows, anywhere but to candles.

Philip Scharper has uttered a prayerful hope for an authentically American theology, one that will speak without a European accent in the American spirit of personal growth, experimentation, and liberty. To that budding Yankee Scheeben or Schmaus, Congar or de Lubac, wherever he is, I shout, "Get a move on!" When he does arrive on the scene, I strongly suspect he will have a thing or two to say, not only about votive candles, but about other forms of exaggeration that the "ad men" in the Church perpetuate under the oriflamme of doctrine. For instance, the references to royalty that pepper our liturgy and devotional literature. There are more peers in our theology tomes than in the pews of Westminster Abbey at a coronation. Kings and queens, knights and counts, crowns, thrones, princes, and all the accouterments of royalty peep out from every page. Tanqueray, not the Italian Riviera, is the real playground of royalty. I wish we could send them all away forever, and let them clutter the casino and beaches of Monaco instead of our theological works.

What has happened to advertising men and to theologians? I think that they have succumbed, in their ultra-enthusiasm, to the incessant jargon of their trade, repeating a certain pattern of ideas until it becomes a meaningless combination of words, completely out of touch with reality and truth. The Living Rosary record cannot change my life. Candles are a long way from being the best of anything. The Bible cannot convert me unless 1) I know what it means, as well as what it says, and 2) unless I apply its doctrine to my daily life. Christ is not a king. He is only symbolically one. Mary is not a queen. She is one only in symbol. When the content of a symbol has been exhausted, its usefulness is at an end and we ought to chuck it out. Such, I contend, is the case with royalty in the Church as well as in the world. To pretend otherwise is to exaggerate, to exalt analogy above truth, to deceive, to be warped by enthusiasm.

Advertising is frequently accused of creating a mythical kingdom of clods—free-wheeling, noisy, grinning, sexy, never-aging creatures in a Technicolor funland that has it over Eden in spades. Such a construct is little worse than a theology that reads like a page from Burke's Peerage. Ad men and theologians have pitched in too enthusiastically, bent on erecting monuments out of their poetic fancies in the misguided belief that they will spur sales. The ad man may have an excuse: his client is seeking the maximization of revenues, as they say. But what about the theologian? Is he so much of an organization man that he is more concerned with image than with truth? Or is he, like the ad man whose potential market cuts across class lines, pitching his appeal to some imagined low intellectual level, and in the process sacrificing logic to emotion and irrelevancy?

Doubtless the Church, and our culture to boot, is in agony today. She has always been. It is one of her distinguishing marks, to suffer. She is a suffering Church. Our aim should be to allay her pangs, to help resolve her human problems, to point out hypocrisy and cant, base materialism and power-madness wherever we see them in her members (starting with ourselves). No good can come from junking the Church and her doctrine as traditionally established. (The metaphor is misleading. One does not "junk" the Church by committing her to a junkyard, but rather by himself moving into the junkyard. If he thinks otherwise, he is a solipsist, or a heretic, or both.) Equally ridiculous, however, is the fellow who tries to minimize the crisis of the Church by shouting rosy messages about her invincibility and divinity, all the while citing statistics from the *Catholic Directory*. He is like the old Jew from Galicia who went to Frankfort, Germany, to visit the magnificent tomb of Amschel Rothschild, founder of the banking family. Stunned by the splendor and costliness of the mausoleum, he could only shake his head and mutter, "That's what I call living!"

CHAPTER 5

Are We Free to Buy?

A state senator from Beverly Hills proposed a brave new law in the California senate early in 1968. His new law would render bartenders liable for auto accidents caused by people who had been drinking, just prior to the accident, in their bars. Some circles might call that law "going to the root of the problem." I would prefer to describe it as a particularly violent manifestation of nincompoopery.

The Spanish Conquistadores have been accused of being in the grip of a daemon: lust for gold. It was probably an Englishman who said it. True or not, daemons do exist, even in our enlightened age. Modern explorers of that murky frontier called "human conduct" are in the possession of their own peculiar daemon. Call it a lust to find the roots of responsibility. At a glance, I should say they are having about as much luck as the Conquistadores out yoo-hooing over the landscape for the Seven Cities of Gold. No one, particularly in the field of jurisprudence, seems to have any idea where he is going in assessing responsibility.

Litigation tells a dreadful story. Survivors of lung cancer victims sue the cigarette manufacturers. Uncle Sam in 1968 awarded $2,534 in lost earnings to a government biochemist who claimed his heart attack was related to the "strain and stress" of his work. A West Palm Beach resident was injured when a rainsoaked pavement collapsed under him. He sued the contractor and the city but a jury ruled that his injuries were caused by an act of God. (The pavement was soaked by a hurricane.) So he sued God. "God is known as the maker of Heaven and Earth and the company is known as his agents, servants and employees who carry on his works as churches." God won the suit. Ralph Nader puts the onus of responsibility for the highway death toll on the automobile makers. Thus the rat race of lawsuits proceeds apace, with no one, so far as I can judge, profiting a whit—except the lawyers.

The confusion in this matter of responsibility is, in large measure, a reflection of our confusion of what constitutes a human act, that is, an act for which a man can be held responsible. And confusion over the nature of a human act springs from muddled thinking about human nature itself. Just who is man? We've come a long way from Feuerbach's "man is what he eats" [1]; a long way from the behavioristic school and from the determinists and environmentalists and regressionists. But the views of these schools continue to influence society. They blamed human conduct on any number of things—except free will. Free will was either ignored or denied. What does this denial do to the question of responsibility? I can hardly be responsible if I have no choice about what I do. If I get drunk and run over someone in my car, it isn't my fault. It's the car maker's. Or the bartender's who sold me the double martinis. Or society's for surrounding me with a hostile environment. Or my nanny's for dropping me on my head when I was a baby. It's everyone's fault, not mine.

Now comes the voice of one crying in the wilderness of

---

[1] This view has lately been revived, but with a twist. If man is what he eats, then in order to understand him, we should study his stool. He is, in fact, his stool. Ask Norman Mailer.

the advertising desert. His name is Vance Packard, and if he doesn't call ad men a brood of vipers, it's not because he's unfamiliar with St. Luke. What has teed Packard off, in particular, is an advertising technique called "motivation research," or MR, for short. MR, by "probing our psyches," uncovers those deepdown, hidden reasons for our acts, tips off the ad man about them and in a sense takes away our freedom not to buy. We are being denied our freedom to buy as we please; we are being seduced by Madison Avenue. Packard calls MR "an invasion of the privacy of our minds." [2] He suspects that ad men are trespassing in our subconscious so that we "do not do what we would do" (Galatians 5:18, with slight pronominal alterations).

Just how much of a menace is MR? Can it take away our freedom to buy or not to buy? Is it a harbinger of 1984 or the latest equivalent of medieval stained-glass windows? At first glance, I confess, it seems to make Orwell a prophet of the highest magnitude. The thought of huge corporations spending upwards of $12 million a year to send psychologists prowling around in our psyches chills me as Bram Stoker never could. I prefer Dracula to these archaeologists of the brain, excavating for motives and then snitching to the advertising people. Perhaps our talisman should be, "Remember the popcorn!" We've all heard by now of the infamous popcorn episode in a New Jersey theater, where popcorn sales were increased 59% by the flashing of subliminal messages on the movie screen.[3] Our very freedom to buy popcorn is under siege. It would appear that MR's assaults on our subconscious are forcing us, all unwilling, to spend too much of our paycheck on products we neither want nor

---

[2] Vance Packard, "The Mass Manipulation of Human Behavior," *America*, Dec. 14, 1957, p. 342.
[3] Subliminal perception is forbidden to television by an amendment to the NAB television code approved June 18, 1958. All TV ads, by this ruling, must be above the threshold of normal awareness. They are well above it, I should say.

can afford. We are being dragged, kicking and protesting, to one sales counter after another by insidious ad men who have our wallets in one hand and the works of Dr. Freud in the other.

Thanks to MR, as Packard has reminded us, sales of the lowly prune have spiraled as its image was changed. When we think of prunes nowadays, we envision big healthy blondes at play instead of pucker-faced old hags complaining of lazy bowels. MR did it. Yes, things look bad. Even the president of the National Foundation for Consumer Credit, S.C. Patterson, has bemoaned the soaring rise of personal bankruptcy on the part of families "that just got in over their heads." [4] Is it conceivable MR is driving one out of every 400 American families into bankruptcy?

Before you dash off an angry letter to your Congressman urging a law outlawing MR, let me make a few remarks. What we have been discussing, as Packard makes clear, is an attack on our *freedom*. But what precisely is free will? When you get to the heart of the matter in analyzing freedom, you discover that you are looking at human intelligence. Intellect and will are not parts of the soul; they are rather two ways of looking at the soul, divided for academic purposes only, just as we distinguish between reason and conscience, or the subjective and objective virtues. The will is a kind of blinkered faculty that locks on to (or chooses) whatever our mind presents to it as choosable. We often think of a bad habit (e.g., impulse buying in a supermarket) as a weakening of the will's power. It isn't a weakening at all. It's just the opposite. The more we indulge a vice, the stronger the will becomes in choosing that vice. What happens is that we inure our minds to showing off vice to the will as eminently worthwhile. Bad

[4] *South Bend Tribune,* April 17, 1968.

side effects (like hell or bankruptcy) are screened off by the intelligence. The more the mind obscures these "side effects," the more readily the will chooses the vice.

We can see the point by returning to Patterson's comments on personal bankruptcy. In addition to noting the increase in the number of families who spend more than they can afford, he also observed that 90% of families who asked for help at credit counseling centers solved their financial problems without resorting to bankruptcy. Now just what did the counseling centers do for these families? They didn't give them calisthenics of the will, or put them on an analyst's couch, or make them write on the blackboard 100 times, "I will not buy impulsively." What they did was to inform their intelligence by showing them, clearly and accurately, the relationship between their income and their outgo. If you make this much, you can only spend so much.

Full freedom, in a very real sense, means a full development of the intelligence. I am free in direct proportion to my ability to consider all aspects of a problem, the merits and demerits of my choice, its ultimate as well as immediate repercussions in my life. A child, for example, enjoys a limited freedom because it cannot ordinarily weigh future goods against present ones. The future has little reality for it.

This is my first point amid the ruckus stirred up by MR: if we exercise intelligence in considering all aspects of buying a product, we will remain free to buy or not to buy, no matter how many wiles the MR witch doctors practice on us. They cannot force us to buy against our will. They cannot change our will from "not buy" to "buy." They can only attempt to influence our intelligence, to alter our view of their product, to make us ignore certain practical handicaps to the buying of a product (like bankruptcy). And this they are doing all the time.

If, as A. C. Nielsen reported, the average American family watched TV 46 hours and 32 minutes per week in the first two months of 1968, think of the commercials it was exposed to. We are daily battered by at least 1,500 advertising messages, and every time we walk into a supermarket, about 8,000 items on those attractive shelves entice us toward the Circe of poverty and bankruptcy. How can we survive? "The same way every organism does which continues to survive: we never tune in on most of it. We exercise selective attention as part of the process of selective perception."[5] Unconsciously we screen off unwanted stimuli and focus only on what fits in with our personal plans of the moment, like a bullfrog calibrating the shape and velocity of the convex forms swooping toward him. Without this selective perception, we would be as wild-eyed and haunted as a hophead on a psychedelic trip. I would go so far as to say that the goal of a truly rational man is to become less, not more, alert to the multitude of stimuli impacting on him from moment to moment. Most of them are irrelevant and trivial at best. And that is my second point: not only do we remain free to buy, but we are protected by the ingenious processes of our nature from the insistent yammering of the commercials. I should like to formulate a law (if Parkinson hasn't already done so) to the effect that the more ads we are exposed to, the fewer we take note of.

Time magazine made reference to selective perception in its cover story on television advertising in the issue of July 12, 1968. Advertising agencies use the acronym CEBUS (Confirmed Exposure but Unconscious) to describe our ability to see a commercial and yet not see or be aware of it at the same time. This precious ability of ours is a

[5] Chester R. Wasson, Frederick D. Sturdivant, and David H. McConaughy, *Competition and Human Behavior* (New York: Appleton-Century-Crofts, 1968), p. 31.

corollary of what is known as the fatigue factor. Now the fatigue factor should not be new to ad men or to *Time* either. Artist and critic Theodore Shaw of Boston has devoted much of his literary life to reminding us of certain commonsense principles often left out of critical discussions. One of them is this inescapable fact: a man will get tired of *any* art work (a Bach chorale, a pop song, or an ad featuring a mechanical stomach) if he is exposed to it often enough. Shaw's *Precious Rubbish,* a remarkably funny and profound work, makes this plain enough. Critics may deplore the revelation, but nothing would so quickly kill all interest in Beethoven and Shakespeare as having their works played on radio and TV all day every day. The human mind can take only so much. Ad men should be forewarned. What we the people want is variety. Variety in life, variety in ads. Why have the realistic Jell-O and Kodak ads, showing commonplace-looking people instead of glamorous models, been so well received? Not because they are superior, but because they are a refreshing change from the ads peopled by excruciatingly beautiful models. But if the ad men give us enough of the plain and simple folk chewing corn-on-the-cob and gulping Jell-O, then we'll soon be clamoring for the glamor guys and gals again. Variety is the key. It is not the spice of life. It *is* life. Even God is a variety (a Trinity) of persons.

If anyone is victimized by motivation research, it is the impulse buyer, that gay shopper who wanders blithely through Marshall (or other) Fields, plucking flowers here and there as the instant, unendurable whim seizes him. He is the prey of the demon impulse, which some spiritual writers at least would prefer to spell IMP-ulse, to stress its satanic origins. The impulse buyer is the anti-paradigm, if you will, of the rational man. He acts without taking into account all or even many of the consequences of his deeds. It's a question, again, of intelligence. And he has been with us from the beginning. I can't believe Adam ate that apple on other than an impulse. Politicians, toy and clothing manufacturers, publishers, and everybody else with something to sell have tried to get us to act on impulse. That's true of the ad man too. But we are as free to reject his advances as we are those of the prostitute, con-man, or demagogue.

Critics who have protested loudest over the implications of MR (Packard, Perrin Stryker, and John P. Sisk, for example) have labeled it an ominous threat to human freedom. The three men I have just cited use almost identical terminology when they ask: Is it right for manufacturers to exploit our human frailties as motives for buying? I think they underestimate us. Are we endowed with a freedom so tenuous and ephemeral that an ad man, with a few psychologically oriented phrases, can snatch it away at the drop of a commercial? I don't think so. Great hurrahs are raised over packaging and image: the image is the message; the package is the product; we are buying the package or the image or the psychological value instead of the product, etc., *ad nauseam*. That may be so in some cases, particularly where products are so much alike that only the image or the package or the ad differentiates one from the other. But if soap won't clean, if cologne doesn't smell right, if a car won't run properly, and if a box of cereal is only half full, then the American won't buy it again, no matter how subtly he is wooed by commercials.

John Sisk has dubbed the ad man who uses MR "Freud in a gray flannel suit." What is more, he has found parallels to MR techniques in Milton's *Paradise Lost,* where the devil tempts Eve. The ad man, with or without MR, "still remains very conspicuously an exploiter of human weaknesses and a dealer in illusions, phantasms and dreams disguised as reality and truth, and for that reason we need to protect ourselves from him." [6] My doubts about Sisk's criticism were seriously aggravated when, further along in the same article, he surveys the mist that surrounds the auto in a Mercury ad and wonders out loud if it might not be ectoplasm. If it is ectoplasm, and not simply a convenient background to highlight the car's styling, then the trance which elicited it belongs to Sisk, not the ad man. Sisk is in a trance, the kind of trance more typical of an art critic, whose very livelihood depends on how well he takes the obvious and evident, say a still life of a bowl of cherries, and discovers vast reservoirs of mystic meaning underneath. (As when John Canaday looks at a portrait of Madame Renoir and sees "the earth goddess.") It is an exercise in whimsy.

I confess I am not greatly worried about motivation research. Vance Packard should be thanked for bringing its existence to our attention, but the suggestion that it is imperiling human freedom has not been proved. If too many people buy more than they can afford, waste money on useless items, sacrifice their children's needs on the altar of their selfish yen for goodies, bankrupt themselves— yes, that is evidence that something is wrong with our society. But it is futile to look at advertising as the source of that malaise. It is another symptom, like divorce, alcoholism, drug addiction. What is wrong with us (and with advertising), and what really worries me, is our belief in Christ's principles and Person, our devotion to rationality. Blaming ad men is an easy out. But it won't hold water. The only way we can heal ourselves is by revitalizing our Christian beliefs, and in particular that tenet which enshrines reason as the font of freedom and human dignity. The problem is an epistemological one. What can we know?

[6] John P. Sisk, "Freud in a Gray Flannel Suit," *America,* Aug. 10, 1957, p. 481.

What can we think? Common sense (and the Pope) reply: the mind *can* reach extra-mental being, *that which is*. (See Paul VI's "The Credo of the People of God," June 30, 1968.) The mind is not hamstrung by being forced to contemplate only its own quintessential navel.

CHAPTER 6

What About Catholic Annuities?

There he stands, looking for all the world like Tony Randall in a black nehru suit. But he is a priest (or rather a drawing of one), and he is holding out to the reader a check (the kind you cash). The type to one side of the ad says, "Suppose *we* send *you* a check for a change!" The italics and the exclamation point, I assume, are intended to stress the anomaly of a priest's giving money to the laity, instead of vice versa. What the ad is inviting us to do is to invest our money with the Catholic Church Extension Society of the U.S.A., "incorporated under the laws of the States of Illinois and Michigan." As of May 29, 1968, the Extension annuity offered a man of age 54 a 5.23% return on his investment of $1,000.

These so-called "Catholic annuities" are heavily advertised. Rev. Father Ralph (is that his real name?) calls his annuity a "mission contract" which will give the investor "high returns depending on age, substantial tax benefits, spiritual remembrances." His annuity, emanating from S.V.D. Catholic Universities in Chicago, offers a 6% return on a $10,000 investment made by a male, age 55. The National Shrine of Our Lady of the Snows purchased an entire page of the May 16, 1968, *Denver Catholic Register* to push its annuity plan. "Put more security in your future with an increase in annual income." Even Father O'Meara, head of the Society for the Propagation of the Faith, is offering "an income you can't outlive," along with "substantial tax reductions."

What are we to think of all this? Our reactions, I suspect, will range from indifference to horror depending upon our view of a profounder question, the relation of money (or capitalism) to Christianity. In introducing that subject, I feel as if I have just uncovered a nest of snakes. Fangs and venom lurk everywhere. But let us proceed, trusting for safety in Providence and plenty of snakebite serum.

It has been about twenty years since the late Thomas Merton enunciated his version of the "dirty money" theory in *Seeds of Contemplation.* What he wrote, and I must pinch myself to believe it, is that a man cannot be a perfect Christian, a saint, unless he is also a communist (small "c"). I have always felt that Tom wrote that sentence as a kind of stimulus to lagging Trappist vocations rather than as a serious blueprint for the revamping of our economic attitudes. I hope so. Ted LeBerthon, among others, has approvingly quoted Merton here, pointing out that the book bears Cardinal Spellman's *Imprimatur.* I don't know what the *Imprimatur* proves, except that Merton's remarks about money do not contradict any defined truth of the Church. But then there aren't really very many defined truths in theology, not nearly so many as one might expect, and none at all, that I can recall, dealing with money. So a man could say almost anything about money and still get an *Imprimatur.* Besides that, the Church has in fact canonized men and women who were anything but communists, who were not squeamish about possessing and using money. To take but one instance, St. Joseph Cafasso, a secular priest, used his money to pay Don Bosco's bills at the end of each month. To aid Bosco's apostolate to boys, Cafasso (again using his own money) bought Bosco a farm for 28,500 lire, a house for 40,000 lire, and left Bosco 50,000 lire in his will. The great Antonio Rosmini also made Don Bosco an "indefinite loan" (meaning he didn't need to pay it back) of 20,000 lire in 1851. If Merton is right in what he said about a saint, then the Church has made a great gaffe in canonizing Cafasso, and we'd better snatch him off the rolls of the saints immediately.

I once wrote an editorial on money which prompted a reader to write one of the most interesting letters I have ever received. In it he so clearly expounds a common Christian view of money that I shall quote the letter in full.

Dear Sir:

One article in your ordinarily excellent paper has caused me to see red; the one in the July 29 issue entitled CREDIT— AT BANK AND IN HEAVEN; featured in minor headlines, but still in major key, SAVE YOUR MONEY—SAVE YOUR SOUL. The headline itself, so far off base, was bad enough; but by the time I had read part way through, my temperature had shot up several notches. It sounded like a Metropolitan Insurance bulletin, and while I can excuse it as being logical in their materialism, I do not understand it in your paper.

The mode of life as extolled in your item runs so contrary to one of the greatest doctrines in all of Christ's teaching, and one of the most difficult for all of us to follow. The doctrine of the PROVIDENCE OF GOD; the consoling fact that our God is a kind and loving and tender Father who knows and anticipates our needs better than we do, who will feed us, clothe us, and shelter us, as we would do for our own children.

"Do not be anxious, saying, 'What shall we eat?' or 'What shall we drink?' or 'What shall we put on?' for your heavenly Father knows that you need all those things."

This is a deceptively hard belief to put into practice; in fact so difficult that those who have successfully done so in the past are today honored as our most glorious saints. While reading your article, I could almost picture the elder Bernardone laying it on thick to his wayward boy. "Now Francis," he was saying, "forget this stuff. Get back to the warehouse. Silk costs money. Don't give it away. Be prudent and save a little bit, or we won't have any for our old age. It's OK to love God and all that, but He doesn't expect us to squander our money on a bunch of beggars."

The height of economic prudence is thoroughly covered in the Sermon on the Mount and nowhere therein can I find any reference to laying a little away in the bank for the future. Yet (and this really burns me up) your author can blithely intone, "It becomes a virtue to save."

You might raise an objection, which wouldn't be new, that it might have been saintly for St. Francis to live from hour to hour depending solely on God's ever-watching care, but he was a single man, and a beggar to boot, with no kids to raise, no taxes to pay, no house to buy, schools to build, etc. And I would answer that the reason none of us parents knows if God will take care of us and our family's needs is because none of us ever tried to let Him with the same spirit and confidence that Francis demonstrated.

We insist on worrying a little bit, too. We're going to provide for that rainy day. That's why I carry hospitalization. But if Francis were alive today, married with a family to raise, I'd wager that he wouldn't have a policy in the house. But he would have unfailing faith, and he would meet his bills better than I do for all my rainy day provisions.

When a new baby comes to our house, do I confidently thank God, knowing that He will protect us, and clothe us, and feed us, provide everything that we really need to enable us to fulfill all of our obligations as parents? Of course, but on the side, I'll sneak over and take out a little more insurance just in case, I suppose, that He doesn't. Now this only shows that I am not practicing this sublime doctrine the way it should be practiced. But at the same time I won't cover up my failings and weaknesses by writing an article extolling an opposite approach to the problem. AND NEITHER SHOULD YOU.

When Christ turned to the tax collector, he said, "Follow me." He could have added, "Bring along a few gold pieces, we'll need them later on." But he didn't. When St. John Bosco needed bread for his boys, he didn't trot down to the bank to draw out some money to buy some. He prayed; and his heavenly Father sent him whatever he needed.

CREDIT—AT BANK AND IN HEAVEN. Nuts! St. Pius was considered a poor credit risk at the bank, but he sure had it in heaven.

The whole point is, your pep talks should be exhorting us to pray the Our Father better. It doesn't do much religious good to present a watered-down version of good business policy. "A $1,000 bill invested will produce little $1 bills." That's true all right, but I dislike reading it on a Catholic editorial page. It sounds like Pius X's exchequer talking, not Pius. And you know which one is the saint.

All that the article will accomplish is to reinforce most of us in some of our pet rationalizations; on why we can pass up a beggar because we can't afford it anyhow, and, anyway, he probably drives a Cadillac after he gets off work, etc.; on why we can put a ten spot in the bank and a dime in the mission plate; and so on. We don't need urging in that direction, it comes easy. You should be telling us something like this: "Therefore, I say to you, do not be anxious for your life, what you shall eat; nor yet for your body, what you shall put on. . . . but seek first the kingdom of God and His justice and all these things shall be given you besides."

Very truly yours,

I have quoted this letter at length, not just because it is so well written, but because it expresses a viewpoint tragically common among Christians today. Like the letter writer, they provide for the future needs of their families (Blue Cross and Blue Shield, insurance policies, mutual funds, etc.) but all the while they look over their shoulder at those Scriptural remarks about Providence and feel guilty as hell.

On a more academic level we run into Cardinal Lercaro's "theology of the poor," which stresses the dignity of poverty as epitomized in the life of Christ. But Christ nowhere praised mere poverty nor did he condemn mere wealth. In Matthew 5:3 he says, "Blessed are the poor in spirit," and in the next verse he adds, "Blessed are the meek." The Greek word for "meek" puts the emphasis not on suffering but on manly resignation to suffering. Suffering alone is of no value unless it is informed by a Christ-like resignation to the will of God. Poverty alone, in similar vein, is of no value unless it is met with Christian fortitude and trust (which means, in my view, that a man is trying as hard as his talents allow to escape it). Could a theology of poverty be evolved after the manner of Christology or ecclesiology? I doubt it, particularly if it is premised on a pejorative view of money. Contemporary intellectuals are in danger of canonizing the poor just as the Romantics canonized the rustic and the child, and as a matter of fact just as priests used to canonize the parents of large families. Thus we have a large number of Christians who look with suspicion on the virtue of couples with few or no children, who think getting back to nature is getting back to God (a kind of "soilvation," you could call it), and who feel guilty about money if they have it and resentful of the wealthy if they do not. Even the rich often fall victim to this guilt complex over money. That may be an additional reason why many of them are seeking public office. It may be they have the naive view that wealth is a fixed sum, so that every dollar I obtain is a dollar out of somebody else's pocket. But wealth is constantly being created. Or again it may be that they seek public office in order to assuage their remorse over having so much money.

Some ecclesiastical writers even look down their noses at people who give only money to the missions or to their parishes. As if that money were not a visible symbol of hours of toil and sacrifice and self-denial, a concretization of spirit, a real part of a man's life! "Who steals my purse steals trash" may scan well, but it is poor philosophy. My purse is a real part of my life, and the man who steals it is stealing part of me, murdering me by inches, just as the

Columbia University student recently was guilty of a kind of homicide when he destroyed a professor's papers which represented a lifetime of study and research.

Writers often have eccentric views of money. Many feel that money kills the muse. Sherwood Anderson was such a one. He pleaded with his publisher to stop sending the $100 weekly advance. "You'll get your book," he exclaimed, "but give me back my poverty." (From *In Friendly Candor* by Edward Weeks) It may be great fun to despise money but it is also impractical. Aelred Carlyle, the extraordinary and weird Benedictine monk, had so great a contempt for money that he left his abbey on Caldey Island in financial chaos, on the brink of bankruptcy, while he himself fled to British Columbia.

Oddly enough I find the attitude of W. Somerset Maugham toward money far more Christian than that of poor Abbot Carlyle or of friend Merton, who lived in financial security in the abbey at Gethsemane, Kentucky. "I had no intention," Maugham has said, "of living on a crust in a garret if I could help it. I had found out that money was like a sixth sense without which you could not make the most of the other five." [1] Great wisdom there, and applicable to anyone but a man with a religious vow of poverty. How I use my money will determine its value to me.

"Do not be anxious," counseled Jesus, about what you eat, or drink, or wear. That's what he said. What did he mean? More precisely, what did he mean by "anxious"? The Greek word *merimna* connotes the idea, not simply of concern, but of over-anxiety or preoccupation. To put it into contemporary slang, "Don't have a nervous breakdown worrying over money." Try not to worry about it at all. But if I conclude that Christ meant we should not be

---

[1] Cited in *Time* magazine, April 27, 1959, p. 94.

concerned at all about money or provision for the future, I will have misinterpreted Matthew 6.[2]

I am reassured in my own blithe prejudices with regard to money by the etymology of the word. "Money" is derived from the Latin "Moneta," a surname of the goddess Juno, in whose temple in Rome money was coined. The word "mint" has the same derivation. It's nice to know the word has a religious origin when the reality it describes is so controverted. Not that Christianity prescribes Capitalism, or any other economic system, for that matter. It is in fact rather skeptical of all such systems since there is ever the danger we may become distracted from our total goal by too deep an immersion in the pursuit of wealth or "success." The operating phrase is "too deep." It would be just as foolish for a man whose duty involves the needs of children to have no concern for money. To those who feel that providing for the future via insurance and savings accounts is evidence of a failure to practice "the sublime doctrine of the Providence of God," let me say that in the New Testament there are as many "capitalist" as "anti-capitalist" texts to be cited. Like the voter who has just watched a heated television debate between political candidates, you will emerge from this tangled problem of faith and finance with your own prejudices intact. So be it. For a deeper study of the matter, you can turn to such authors as David McCord Wright, who in *Modern Age* (Fall, 1957) attempts to find a Christian approach to economic systems.

With all that under our belts, we can return to the Catholic annuity ads which unashamedly recommend investing for the future. If, like my letter-writing critic, you

---

[2] See, for example, *The Vocabulary of the Greek Testament* by Moulton-Milligan, p. 398; or *A Catholic Commentary on Holy Scripture,* Dom Bernard Orchard, general editor, pp. 863, 864. I think it goes without saying that an individual should be extremely cautious about buttressing his views with quotations from the Scriptures. One needn't be a Greek scholar to read the Bible profitably. But it helps avoid a lot of misconceptions.

believe God wants us to pray in lieu of investing in securities, then such ads will be totally uncongenial to you. If, on the other hand, you think Christ did not abrogate common sense along with the Old Law, you will suspend your verdict until the evidence is in.

An inquiry to the Oblate Fathers at the Shrine of Our Lady of the Snows, Belleville, Ill., produces a spate of literature, featuring a handsome, 16-page brochure entitled "Answers to Questions about Safe Investments, Sound Investments & Secure Investments in Life Income Annuity Contracts." The strictly commercial note sounded by the title quickly disappears once we go inside the booklet. We are greeted there by a photo of the tower of the shrine church, a kind of exaltation of parabolic arches from which thrusts a needle-like shaft. The cross atop the shaft (I read no symbolism here) is barely discernible. Throughout the remainder of the text we are presented with a series of questions and answers about annuities which are woven through photographs of the stations of the cross. I don't know why the fathers chose the stations for use in this brochure, but to a cynic they could be mortally distressing. The reply to the question about withdrawal of the principal is directly opposite the second fall of Jesus. And just below the statement that annuity payments are made twice a year (unless otherwise specified) Jesus is buried in the tomb. What we are viewing is a typographical and theological wedding of investment and religion, and the text reinforces that conviction. "By investing in a Life Income Annuity Investment Contract," we read on page seven, "you can *see* your investment at work and you can *know* that you have gained merit in Heaven for good works during your lifetime" (italics in text). And again, "Moreover, you become a perpetual member of the Society called the League of Mary Immaculate. This enables you to merit many spiritual benefits." (In case you are not satisfied, that is, by being merely a member of the Church.) This second quotation, incidentally, is all underlined in red ink, perhaps a tacit reminder of what can happen to you if you don't invest wisely, red being the color of deficits as well as of hellfire. On the back cover of the booklet, under a drawing of an hourglass, the Oblate Fathers sum up their case: "Invest in eternity today, while there is yet time."

Father Ralph of S.V.D. Catholic Universities, in his pamphlet entitled "How to Invest Wisely," makes pretty much the same pitch. He writes on page five: "Lifetime protection is yours and the added spiritual satisfaction, knowing that you are sharing actively in the world's noblest work—that of saving souls for eternity." The booklet issued by the Extension Society and called simply "Extension Annuities" stimulates our confidence in its investment program by quoting praises of the Society from Pope John XXIII and Pope Paul VI, though it is not made clear whether or not they have purchased annuities.

Reading such stuff may make it hard for you to keep your choler buttoned down. Most of us probably feel some distaste over these contrapuntal orchestrations of God and mammon. It has ever been thus. Nestorius and the legions of his intellectual heirs were scandalized by the thought of the Savior being truly man, having to eat and such, so they denied his humanness. Similarly, the thought of a human Church (as well as divine), one that has to eat, strikes a sensitive nerve and we are tempted to wish that the Church were totally spiritual or invisible. We may even envision the Church as having been freed not only from persecution but also of her spirituality (that is, her lack of ecclesiastical riches) by Constantine in the fourth century. And like all good antiquarians, we may wish that she could return to that pristine age of pain and poverty— or at least of poverty. But historically "by the end of the third century it may be said that collective ownership of wealth by the Church was an accomplished fact." [3] At least one persecution, that of Valerian in 257, was motivated in part by the State's lust for the great wealth of the Church. And this a half century before Constantine, during the very era of the heroic martyrs!

Another popular view is to say: "Well, most of us lukewarm Christians compromise in matters of money, but at least the saints practiced the genuine virtue of poverty as Christ taught we should." Take Phyllis McGinley, whose verses about the saints are the delight of us all. She has lately delivered herself of a definition of "saint." They were "men and women who take the Gospels literally." [4] Guess which passage from Scripture she cites, not once but twice? The one about selling all we have and giving to the poor and following you know Who. She is saying, then, that *all* the saints sold, gave, and followed. In proof of which she lists a number who did (Francis of Assisi, the Desert Fathers, Martin, William Pinchon, Cyran the Abbot, Vincent Pallotti, Laurence O'Toole and Pius X).

It is considered bad manners to deny a major premise, particularly a woman's, but it must be done. It is simply untrue to say that all the saints gave away their possessions. If Miss McGinley means that the saints did not use their money to live in luxury, she is right. If she means that they did not possess any money, she is dead wrong. Many saints did not, especially those with a vow of poverty; for them to have possessed money would have been a violation of their vow. But the saints who had no such vow did, in many cases, possess money. Joseph Cafasso is but one example. Vincent Pallotti, whom she cites as having come home "half naked" a number of times after giving his clothes to the poor, had lots of money. He inherited it from his father.

---

[3] Henri Daniel-Rops, *The Church of Apostles and Martyrs* (Garden City: Doubleday, 1962), Vol. II, p. 43.

[4] "What Is a Saint?" *The Critic,* June-July, 1968, p. 35.

But he used it, not to buy lavish furniture and clothing and food, but to advance the cause of the Church, as for instance when he endowed (with funds left him in his father's will) the Home of the Sacred Heart, a girls' orphanage in Rome. By a strange paradox, the deeply spiritual man who in his books spoke of ecclesiastical wealth as the "fifth wound" of the Church, who recommended that the Church be taxed, this same man, Antonio Rosmini, in 1820 inherited an estimated 500,000 pounds, about $2 million, which he devoted to pious uses such as his already mentioned loan to Don Bosco.[5]

I agree with Miss McGinley that we need saints today to "lead us out of the onrushing night that so threateningly descends." Hence, the question of what a saint really is seems vitally important. Wrong notions cause the most frightful havoc among those who try to imitate their lives. Can one imagine a father of seven selling all he has in order to follow Christ? What about the children? Who will pay for their eye operations, their flu shots, their hospital bills, their clothes? Will that father be found on picket lines or in jail, as Miss McGinley hints a saint would be in this our day? I can't believe it. He should rather be doing his duty, as husband and father, as heroically as possible. That is the essence of holiness. There is no doubt of the value of reading Butler's *Lives of the Saints,* that vast compendium of facts about all the saints who ever lived—and a few who didn't. But to get a correct idea of the essence of holiness, one should rather consult Benedict XIV's *De servorum Dei beatificatione et beatorum canonizatione.* More clearly than any other work it shows not only those qualities a saint was canonized *because of* but those qualities he was canonized *in spite of.* It is not always easy to know which is which. Was Pius X raised to the altars because he took snuff? Or the Little Flower because of her narrow view of the

[5] Claude Leetham, *Rosmini* (Baltimore: Helicon Press, 1957), p. 26.

world? Or John Baptist Rossi because he nearly ruined his health by imprudent fasting as a young man?

It is the spirit, not the fact, of poverty which characterizes the saints. This spirit is perhaps most often violated in our own time by over-elaborate and too expensive ornamentation of rectories, convents, and monasteries; by the silly custom of bishops' living in posh homes and riding around in limousines (is their divinely given apostolic authority in need of such symbols?), and in general by the too luxurious style of living of the clergy (including monks and friars).

When Francis of Assisi gave away his food, clothes, and books he was, says Miss McGinley, "following a trail as old as Christendom." True enough. But is that why he was canonized? Or more to the point, must I do that in order to be a saint? No. There are saints who did not. Let him who can, invest in a Catholic annuity without fear of going counter to the canons of sanctity. Better that than giving away everything and becoming a ward of the State. The money invested will be put to good use in the maintenance of hospitals, seminaries, and missions. So write to Rev. Father Ralph or to the others. Alms-giving is still a meritorious act, even that sophisticated variety of modern times which involves 6% interest and income tax benefits.

But I do wish that the men who write those Catholic annuity brochures would pay more attention to the niceties. I wish Father Edwin Guild in Belleville would not, in his follow-up letter to my inquiry, assure me at the end that he will remember me in his Mass tomorrow. That smacks of simoniacal bribery. I wish that Rev. Father Ralph would not say that investing in his "life income mission contract" will free me from "all worries." It won't. It can't. And above all, let them all desist from those abominable statements to the effect that my investment here is ringing heaven's cash registers. They don't know that and neither do I. The spiritual value of any action of mine (including this form of alms-giving) depends on the love and grace with which I perform it. No one knows the depth of those qualities save God. And He isn't telling anyone.

Let them continue to offer their annuities. Let the Protestant sects continue to put us into their retirement homes at the price of our life savings. They are giving the aged some security in a perilously inflationary age. But at the same time let no one tell me I will be a saint for my investment. And let no one tell me I am a devil for it either, or unworthy, or unChristian.

I can't imagine that my message will be popular in some quarters. Not when bishops are declaring moratoriums on church building so that the money can be spent on the poor. Not when bishops try to give away parish buildings to Federal poverty programs, obviously overestimating the apostolic enthusiasm of the bureaucrats. Not when Archbishop Casey of Denver announces in his diocesan paper that he will give $1 million to the needy, under the delusion, I suppose, that it is his money to give. The mania many men have today to give away other people's money to the poor amounts to an epidemic. Such monies may be well spent if they are used on programs like job-training and education. But you can't buy virtues of any sort, not loyalty, not truth, not hard work, not thrift, not honesty. You can't force a man to be unpoor. I have lived in a ghetto since 1963 and therefore assume that my view of it is relatively "from the bottom." I have found no preponderance of saints down here, no Lake Meades of dignity and virtue to put the despised suburbs to shame. If I have learned anything, it is that the dignity of the poor has been systematically stripped away by our welfare system of doles. The State's doles have never worked. And now the Church wants to follow suit! It is an irony I can't understand.

Meanwhile, as the State assumes more and more of the burden of "charity" once borne by the Church, as taxes mount up above the level once described by moralists as just, and as inflation makes money worth less and less, is it surprising that Christian groups must resort to such measures as annuities and retirement homes in their search for money? I say, more power to them. And as for me, well, I'll take whatever measures are needed to see that as much of my money as possible ends up in the hands of the Church, my relatives, and my friends, and as little as possible in the probate courts, the Federal government, and its rapacious echelons of bureaus. I may even buy an annuity or two —if I ever have the money.

CHAPTER 7

Sex, Soap, and Liturgy

The wise advertising man will make a careful study of the Church, for its mission is in a sense the selling of a product and involves a number of propaganda techniques. Thanks to Herr Goebbels, "propaganda" has become a dirty word, but it needn't be. Through the efforts of journalists, a considerable number of dirty words has evolved in past years, and for the benefit of ad men, who are enamored of words, I should like to list a few of them, a kind of contemporary devil's dictionary which shows how words can be debased. "Dogma" is a dirty word. So is "prejudice." (If it is modified by the term "racial," it ranks as today's equivalent of the unforgivable sin against the Holy Ghost.) "Conservative" is a dirty word, and "German," and "Anglo-Saxon." "Roman" used to be a derogatory adjective among some Protestants when used to modify "Catholic." Nowadays it is being used by certain far-out Catholics in pejorative reference to the traditional ecclesiastical structure of the Church. "Inequality" is becoming a dirty word, as the equalitarians rush us along the road to that cloudcuckooland of absolute sameness. Only the other day the local sports pages reported that a lawyer for the N.F.L. players' association (something to do with football) attempted to justify raising the minimum season's wage (for about eight months' work) from $10,000 to $15,000. His logical process sheds wondrous light on the modern scene. In speaking of the "hungry" $10,000 per-year athlete, he said, "And his wife has got to sit alongside Cherry [Mrs. Bart] Starr, who's out in a new coat. That player may be hungry, but he's not going to be happy." If he is hungry at a wage of $10,000 per year, then surely it's his appetites and not his wages that need adjusting. Must all players' wives get new coats at the same time to keep team morale at a high pitch? Ah equality!

Through manifold propaganda techniques, then, the Church tries to sell men on its product, which is the total integration of humans into divine life through Christ. It makes use of words (both inspired and tedious), music and singing, colorful visual displays, and symbols of all sorts. The individual who first used the word "psychedelic" under the impression he was describing something new had never been to a pontifical Mass or to a canonization ceremony in Rome. I was even going to describe Christ as the ideal ad man, but I felt the analogy would offend Dan Herr so I scuttled it. How have some churchmen attempted to sell a part of their "product," in this case, the liturgy?

In a 1954 interview at Regis College, Denver, the late Gerald Ellard, S.J., discussed with me the liturgical movement, to which he made notable contributions. "As it is now," he remarked, "the Mass makes very poor provision for spectator appeal. It should have the appeal of a football game or a prizefight." I should imagine Father Ellard would have been quite at home in the November celebration of the god Osiris in ancient Rome, a regular carnival of participation to the piping of flutes and the rattle of *sistra*. Is that what the Church wants?

Father Ellard's statement reflects a misconception that has returned to haunt liturgists and is afflicting much contemporary advertising. What is wrong here is that we are being encouraged to buy a product for the wrong reasons. There has been a confusion of ends, a characteristic illness of our society. We see it everywhere: the collegian who thinks his duty is the reformation of the social and political order; the politician for whom elective office is a means of personal enrichment; the TV comedian who fancies himself an expert on philosophy and foreign policy. Not only have men confused their duties or roles, but they have confused the functions of the things around them. Collegiate sport has been degraded into badly disguised professionalism, a minor league for professional sport. Nature (by which I mean the fields and forests) is no longer considered a place where city men get away from routine. It has become a font of almost everything: reason and faith (Emerson); calm, sure, and deep thoughts and an awareness of "a presence mightier than any human fellowship" (Donald Culross Peattie); soul-healing renewal (Paul Friggen); a better knowledge of God (Dr. Tom Dooley); knowledge of one's self and of God (Justice William O. Douglas); and even mystical insight into our primordial roots (Joseph Wood Krutch).

The number of advertisements that confuse the ends of the products is legion. Each of us has his own pet list. One thinks at once of the soft drink which, when it washes down my gullet, will assimilate me into the mainstream and not leave me "out in the warm." And there are the hair rinses, toothpastes, and deodorants which are placarded as guarantees of sexual adventure. This wholesale dragging of genitalia into the world of the commercial has raised more hackles than taxes or Charles de Gaulle. But hackle-raising as the sex pitch is, I object to it because it is philosophically unsound, because it confuses the ends of the products. Toothpaste has some sort of relationship to dental caries, but none at all to sexual conquest. Automobiles are essentially a means of moving from one place to another. To present them in advertising as billboards of personal distinction, diving boards into sex experience, tools for demonstrating bravery, or outlets for existential frustration is to confuse ends again, and to doom the consumer's hopes by promising him something the product can't deliver.

That is, in essence, what happened with the liturgy. Back in 1956–57, many liturgists wrote so enthusiastically of the miracles which would occur with the new Holy Week ritual that one was led to expect a tidal bore of heroic virtue to sweep across the face (faith) of the earth. But the faithful were exposed to the rearrangement of the accidental furniture of the liturgy, and what happened? There was no miracle, no abrupt explosion of faith, and the liturgists, already a deeply gloomy lot, wept and gnashed their teeth. What is worse, they began to look about for new changes which would, in the words of Vatican II, "draw the faithful into the compelling love of Christ and set them afire" (*Constitution on the Sacred Liturgy*). And so the emphasis on worship at Mass, to single out one part of the liturgy, has shifted from the Missal, to the dialogue Mass, to the sung Mass, to the Mass facing the people, to the vernacular Mass, to the folk and guitar Mass—and all in the misplaced hope that these external, accidental alterations will produce a modern Cana, turning the water of spiritual mediocrity into the wine of universal sanctity. How many conscientious laymen have meekly submitted to the liturgical innovations under the delusion they would be suddenly revivified in their faith and begin to vibrate to the Mass and sacraments the way a soccer fan vibrates to World Cup play.

All this holy tinkering with the mechanics of worship has not brought back the lost sheep, or converted the luke-warm. If you are saddened at that, then you were led to expect too much from the liturgical changes. "You cannot be a fully Catholic Christian woman unless you sing the songs of the Church," said Ermine Vitry, O.S.B., back in the 50's to a group of CCD women. Merton said we had to be communists; now Vitry says we must be singers. Where will it all end? How did those women feel when their choral participation did not appreciably change the realities of their spiritual life? I should imagine they were as disappointed as the woman who bought a certain detergent in the belief that by sticking her husband's dirty overalls into it she would earn him immediate promotion from his job of wiping down diesel locomotives. The ad men for both detergent and liturgy have fallen into unnatural vice and "given up the truth of God for a lie" (Romans 1:35). Not in a doctrinal or moral sense but in a philosophic one. For the "truth" of even so mundane a creature as detergent or toothpaste embraces the purposes for which it is made. Unlike St. Paul, I will not say that ad men, on account of this perversion of reality, are "deserving of death." But I do recommend that they go on a pilgrimage to Canossa, in this case, any business college, where they be required to take a semester of business ethics. That should be penance enough.

If they persevere in their present course, promising too much from the use of their product or exaggerating its benefits, then their soda pop or hair rinse will suffer the same fate as the liturgy: disappointed users will begin to abandon it. Daniel Callahan wrote what must be the most poignant and tragic commentary yet on the terrible disenchantment felt by a man who had been led to expect too much from the liturgical changes. After first noting that the alterations in the liturgy had not brought off the expected miracles of faith and charity, Callahan wrote:

> Should we continue believing that the liturgy is, in the words of the Council [Vatican II], "the center and the source of the Christian life"?

I want to argue that it should be nothing of the kind. *The primacy of place accorded the liturgy is one of the most important sources of the Church's failure to carry out its Christian work and witness in the world.*[1] (His italics)

I imagine that like a lot of us he had been waiting for the people of God to combust in white-hot flames of Christian love just as soon as the liturgy was changed, for isn't that what many of the liturgists said would happen? When the miracle didn't come off, Callahan decided that if it couldn't do the job, it should be lowered in our scale of values and put "not at the top and very possibly not even near the top."

His argument for the demotion of Mass and sacraments (= liturgy) runs as follows: Millions of people without the liturgy live good lives. Many with access to the liturgy do not so live. Therefore, the liturgy is obviously irrelevant to true virtue. We might just as well argue: Millions of the citizens of India enjoy good health. Millions of Americans die of disease. Therefore, we Americans should junk our vast programs of medical care and research (they obviously aren't doing the job) and invest the money in something more worthwhile, say, a few thousand head of sacred cattle.

Everyone has at one time or another wished that there were something in the spiritual life that would do what gibberellic acid does in the vegetable kingdom, making cabbages shoot up twelve feet in height, flowers bloom early, and strawberries have five times the normal number of runners. But we must face reality: there must first elapse that "allotted time." How many parents have scolded their children for not acting like adults? But the acorn is not the oak and will not become so until its allotted time is fulfilled. Detergents are not the gibberellin to speed up promotions.

[1] *The National Catholic Reporter*, Aug. 7, 1967, p. 5.

Liturgical adjustments are not the gibberellin that will make the mustard seed of faith bust out all at once into a full-fledged tree. There must first be that allotted time. As a South Carolina preacher put it, "The Lord—He takes His time. He ain't no hurry-up Lord. He waits! Yes, He waits and He does it right . . . the Lord moves at His own speed." [2]

I think someone misinformed Mr. Callahan about the liturgical changes, grossly exaggerating the effects they would produce and the speed with which they would transform life. Therein lies the tale. Misinformation is the bane of the Church as it is of the advertising world. Leading people on to false expectations is deluding them. Perhaps the use of figurative language in describing the fruits of the liturgy ("fires of love," "burning charity") is defective, even, or especially, when used by the Pope. But the Pope is not infallible in matters of rhetoric. And I should think that a mature grounding in dogmatic theology would enable a Catholic to put that grandiloquent prose in its proper light and to keep in mind that spiritual maturation is a hard won and gradual process, an evolution if you like, that the liturgy (Mass and sacraments) can assist more powerfully than anything else, but that nothing on earth can make it occur instantaneously.

The ad man has no ecumenical councils, doctrinal theses, liturgical constitutions, or de fide dogmas to guide him. Only the light of his common sense and personal moral code. But these should be enough to show him that a hair lotion cannot assure popularity nor Pepsodent a movie contract. And surely the liturgist will recognize that an English Mass, complete with bugia candles, double genuflections, and flawless singing of neums and quilismas will not insure instant and universal charity. Nor will putting the Credo to

[2] William Price Fox, "Down in 'The Hard Lard Belt,'" *TV Guide,* July 6, 1968, p. 7.

the tune of "Jambalaya" with Glen Campbell at the guitar do a bit more.

"There is no such thing as the hard sell or the soft sell. There is only the smart sell and the stupid sell." Thus spoke Charles Brower of Batten, Barton, Durstine, and Osborn, a New York ad agency. I hope sincerely that advertising men do not buy the philosophy underlying Brower's regrettable remark. What he is saying is that the end (sales) justifies the means (any pitch that will increase sales). A more useful and a more ethical dictum would be: whether the sell be hard or soft, it should be true. And true means, among other things, that it will not promise that the product will give what of its nature it cannot deliver. Using Vote toothpaste will not guarantee a happening in your bathroom. Liturgical adjustments will not suddenly make people substitute "brotherhood of man" for the more popular, if less Christian, "botherhood of man."

In a lucid and probing article on the liturgy, Robert Ostermann has written:

> I wonder, too, why contempt for the office of teaching is so popular? You can hardly go into a liturgical discussion without hearing the protest—But doctrine doesn't make one holy. I would like to hear queried a little more often, if holiness is not doctrine lived? [3]

Holiness is doctrine lived. That remark should be engraved in our memories. In an age that lionizes men who dream and who have visions; in an age when presidential aspirants who campaign on ideological grounds are said to have no chance of winning; in an age when sensation and random experience of stimuli are regarded as wellsprings of understanding and truth—in such an age, one wonders if there is any room left for doctrine. The Pope evidently thinks that there is, as even

---

[3] Robert Ostermann, "The Spirit and the Letter of Worship," *The Catholic World*, May, 1956, p. 94.

a quick look at the decrees of the Second Vatican Council will show. Sound advertising, like an integral Christian life, must likewise be based on information, not on bits of inspiration. The truth cannot set you free unless you make it your own. Knowledge is the basis of virtue; knowledge is mandatory for success in one's daily life or in the formulation of an ad for a hoola hoop. Knowledge is the answer to Daniel Callahan's painful dilemma over the liturgy.

But isn't this emphasis on knowledge exalting head over heart? Haven't we had enough head? Isn't what we need now the proclamation of the primacy of heart, of love? I have no objection to extolling the merits of heart (or even of kidneys, liver, or spleen). The heart is the symbol of love, and love has never been a glut on the market. But love is a habit of the will and as such is under the control of the intellect. Freedom, as we already saw, depends directly on intelligence. So does love. Isn't it said that one cannot love what he doesn't know? And listen to St. Paul as he writes his converts in Philippi: "I pray that your love may more and more abound in knowledge and all discernment" (1:9). Yes, we need love, but we need a love abounding in knowledge.

One cannot love God unless he studies (in whatever way his life and talents best allow) who God is; unless he familiarizes himself with God's biography. And one cannot love the liturgy unless he first studies to know what it is and what it can do. If his knowledge is defective, his love will be defective.

We must not make the Catholic religion seem formalistic, or *kibishii,* as the Japanese put it. In past centuries, perhaps, there was some such tendency, too great a stress on "thou shalt not's," a proneness to interpret Christ and His word in legalistic and juridical terms. Scholars like Professor Arnold of Tübingen trace this tendency to the catechism of

St. Peter Canisius in the 16th century. (Apparently there
is much comfort to be derived from assigning blame for
things, otherwise why would we spend so much time doing
it?) Whether Peter must bear this onus or not, be does
deserve great credit for other achievements, not least of
which was his effort to base Christian virtue on dogmatic
truth. Holiness is doctrine lived. If the doctrine is faulty,
what will happen to the holiness? Peter was not the first
to base virtue on true knowledge of God. Listen to this
description of St. Ambrose:

> . . . he was pre-eminently interested in practical religion. It was
> the Christian life he had in view; and his labours in the sphere of
> Christian thought were occasioned by his conviction that right
> thinking is the indispensable condition of right living. . . . it
> was the Christian life that he had chiefly in view. He did not seek
> to be original or subtle or profund; his aim was to furnish men of
> average common sense with a sound doctrinal foundation
> whereon they could safely build the structure of practical
> religion.[4]

Studying doctrine is not externalizing our faith, as some
claim, but rather internalizing it, making its truths a part of
our intellectual and moral outlook. How else can they influence our conduct? Knowledge is not virtue. Professors
are not thereby saints. But of the sins committed by good
men in ignorance and bad men in malevolence, the former
are the greater danger. We are on our guard against the
latter.

Ironically we arrive at a solution to the misplaced emphasis and distortion of advertising, whether of liturgy or
soap, in one of those dirty words we met at the beginning
of the chapter. The word is "dogma." It means simply
"teaching," that is, the truths taught by Christ to His
Church, and living in it, in its traditions and in its sacred

[4] Frederick Homes Dudden, *St. Ambrose, His Life and Times* (London:
Oxford at the Clarendon Press, 1935), Vol. II, p. 556.

Words. It is unlikely that a Christian ad man who is ignorant of Christ's message will write responsible copy. The perversions we encounter in advertising may very well be an effort by a copywriter to substitute for the truth (which he may not know) some other quality such as change, or shock, or cute deception, or his own version of j. n. d. (that "just noticeable difference" that makes an ad catch our eye). Unable to recognize who his audience is, and why it is, unable to think of men in terms of the Incarnation and Redemption, he debases them by his cheap message, inferring that his product is their destiny, that it will bring them salvation and peace and exorcize forever the demons of dissatisfaction, frustration, anxiety, and emptiness. Knowledge, the foundation of virtue, would save him from such hopeless voyages into intellectual vacuity. Of him can be said what critic Alfred Kazin once remarked of the American dramatist:

> To be a "rebel" is easy. To grow a beard, to be sexually brave, to take dope, even to kill—all these are understood experiences of "nonconformism." The one thing you cannot do is think, i.e., to build on your private definition of the world, and so to enjoy what Thomas Mann called the "wealth of the mind"—that which makes a writer feel that he has the world in his hand.[5]

And if our definition of man and of the world is not our private one, but rather the ineffable definition of God-made-man, then we do indeed have the world in our hands, and no one can prize it away from us.

[5] Quoted in *Time* magazine, June 6, 1960, p. 67.

CHAPTER 8

Is TV Ruining Your Child?

Perhaps you saw that precious photograph of Allen Funt, late of "Candid Camera," wearing his fedora upside down to the delight of a giggling child. Mr. Funt, to judge from his public statements, is one of the most notable living believers in Rousseau's doctrine of the romantic exaltation of childhood. But I will let him speak for himself:

> Children are people before they've been ruined. They have a purity of mind, a purity of motive—not necessarily unselfish, but pure. They look at the world out of their own eyes. You ask them about love, beauty, truth, and their answers are original, creative. The child's mind has a purity of *thought*. He's unique. He's an individual.
>
> Where do we lose this individuality? I don't know. Early. We lose it early in life. At 6 or 7 you already see the children collecting prejudices from the parents. The schools destroy their originality. They give the children predigested thinking, prefabricated values. By the time they're grown, they're full-fledged members of the herd. They're no longer unique. They're conformists who'll walk up a "down" escalator, because six other guys are doing it.[1]

Mr. Funt must judge childhood from the children he has met and known and loved and been around. So do I.

[1] *TV Guide,* June 22, 1963, p. 20.

Therefore, one of two things has occurred: either we have been exposed to two entirely different species of child (which I doubt), or else he accepts that rosy philosophy of childhood as the golden age, that time of unspoilt purity, spontaneity, individuality, honesty, and probity—Rousseau's view.

Whatever else we may say of children, they are decidedly innocent. But "innocent" does not denote purity or virtue or character. It means, quite literally, "harmless." The word "innocuous" comes from the identical Latin root. An innocuous person is one who has no effect, for good or for ill, on those around him. A child, forgive me for saying so, perfectly fulfills that definition. That is why asking children for their opinions on truth or beauty or justice, or almost anything else, is such frightful nonsense. Innocence means a child has no vices, true enough. But with equal force it means he has no virtues. He is not able to perform acts which can be called truly and completely human, as moral theologians (and W. C. Fields) have noted in the past.

That is not what Rousseau taught. He maintained that civilization had imposed a set of forms upon man which intruded between him and true love, true genius, true spontaneity, true worship. To obtain a return to these pure and unspoiled virtues, he said we must look for an individual who has not been contaminated by civilization. But who would that be? Answered Rousseau, a barbarian in the uncivilized wilderness, or a rustic far out on the unsullied farm, or a child. And the other Romantics parroted this line of thought. Maeterlinck said that the wisdom of a child's passing remark outweighs all the wisdom of the ages. Wordsworth addressed the child as a "mighty prophet! Seer blest!" "Wherever children are," wrote Novalis, "there is the golden age." To the Romantics, and to Allen Funt, the child is no longer a half-grown man or woman, the young of our species, but the archetypal holy innocent, whose joy and unthinking wisdom we should try to recapture, if only for a moment, whose happiness irradiates a lost world. So the cult of childhood begins.[2]

The cult of childhood begins, all right, but at a time when we should have expected it. That is, in our own age (or non-age) which idolizes non-heroes, non-books, non-art, and non-sense. Now we can add to these non-entities an addition: the non-person, that is, the child. "What is not is the only thing that is beautiful," Rousseau claimed. What *is,* we may conclude, is ugly. Children *are not;* I mean they are shapeless, potential, becoming, struggling for form. To anyone then, who shares Rousseau's views, children are beautiful, inspiring, and oracular. They are touchstones of wisdom, delphic soothsayers who can lead us at last into that lotus land of unpredigested and unprefabricated truth—whatever that is.

Before we can begin to discuss the influence on children of television commercials, we had better understand what a child is. He is both more and less than we expect. He is less because he is not, *pace* Mr. Funt, "father to the man," or prophet, or seer, or oracle in the playpen. He is a repository of possibilities, not an enlightened philosopher of the transcendentals. To borrow from the language of Anaximander, the child is a kind of human *Urstoff,* that is, a boundless, indeterminate hunk of potentiality from which most anything can evolve. His most noteworthy quality (and here I agree with Rousseau) is his ignorance. Now if, like Rousseau, a man esteems ignorance, he is a devotee of the cult of childhood. If not, he had better look elsewhere for inspiration and example.

Mr. Funt says that children are nonconformists. Yet anyone who has observed them closely, at work or at play,

2 J. B. Priestly, *Literature and Western Man* (New York: Harper, 1960), p. 118.

has discovered that they are notorious copycats, and they themselves recognize it for the word is a part of their vocabulary from earliest days. When we speak of a natural leader (or "opinion leader," as Paul Lazarsfeld terms him), we refer to an individual whose strength of personality draws others to him and governs their tastes and modes of action. Such a creature is as rare among children as he is among adults.

But a child is also more than we expect. Christ praised childhood. "Unless you are converted and become like little children, you shall not enter the kingdom of heaven" (Mt 18:3). What on earth did He mean? We cannot become innocent again, nor should we wish to. We cannot unlive our lives. But God never demands the impossible. Perhaps our Lord was referring to ambition, surely not a fault of children, and to the devious politicking by which ambitious men, in the Church and out of it, establish eminence and power as their goals. Children are open and almost painfully undissimulating, virtues we could well emulate. More importantly, they are simple, in the sense that they do what they are doing (*age quod agis*), even if they have as yet no clear vision of which tasks take precedence. And lest we forget, they are shrewd, cunning, and persistent in having their own way, a fact which sometimes bewilders permissive parents and teachers, but which merely reflects an earlier point, namely, that they are potential creatures desperately in need of formation.

How do TV commercials affect children? How, in other words, does TV in general affect them, since I doubt they make any clearcut distinction between the program and the sponsor's message. Some critics, especially since the assassinations in Dallas, Memphis, and Los Angeles, have asserted that television gives our children basic training in techniques of violence, that it teaches the child force as a means of solving problems. Others believe that TV is producing a bumper crop of materialistic, sensual, non-thinking hedonists, disturbed myopiacs with no interest in reading, studying, or the "finer things." I hear in these views echoes of Pope Gregory the Great, writing to the Patriarch of Constantinople in 595 A. D., "The last hour is come." But we are still here, and will be in another 1500 years, even if television bears a closer resemblance to Attila the Hun than I give it credit for. There is no doubt that TV influences children. The question is: How? In what way? Is there any scientific method for measuring its effect?

The best study of this problem that I know of was carried out by three British sociologists, whose conclusions, incidentally, have a rather optimistic tinge.[3] They made a three-year study of 4,500 children, aged 10 to 14, children who spent an average of two hours a day looking at television. What they found out should give parents hope, but it will not relieve television writers and ad men of their responsibilities. The results, in brief:

1) If a child has access to more than one channel, he will have little contact with programs that broaden his tastes. He will follow the path of least resistance and watch only what he likes.
2) Westerns, even those with violence, frightened only the very young and insecure child. Apparently the stylized form of the Western and the ritual survival of the hero made the violence seem unreal.
3) Detective, murder, and crime thrillers were often mentioned as frightening by both adolescents and children. The violence was more realistic to them than that in the Westerns.
4) Many children were frightened by horror programs and science fiction thrillers. Yet oddly enough, real events of a violent nature, such as those seen in newsreels, were seldom mentioned by the children as frightening.
5) Guns and anything to do with guns proved *least* frightening to the children. Most frightening were daggers and sharp instruments, with swords coming somewhere in between. Fictional

[3] Hilda Himmelweit, A. N. Oppenheim, and Pamela Vince, *Television and the Child* (London: Oxford University Press, 1958).

fistfights were less disturbing than those in real life, as in a sports show, for instance.

6) Verbal acts of aggression, reprimand, and ridicule sometimes occasioned more unease in the children than physical aggression. The children seemed most disturbed by situations with which they could not identify themselves, a more important factor, evidently, than the amount of violence shown. "Children enjoy being a little frightened; they like suspense for the sake of the relief that follows. There is a narrow margin between pleasurable suspense and intolerable fear." (p. 19)

7) Television shows are unlikely to cause aggressive behavior, except possibly in children who are emotionally disturbed. There is, however, no evidence that programs of violence help the children in any way.

8) For the most part, television viewing proved neither a help nor a hindrance to the child's general knowledge and school performance, except for the very young or duller students (as yet able to read very little) for whom it was a definite advantage, giving them information at a suitable pace in dramatic and visual form.[4] The brighter and older children suffered, however, because TV viewing gave them nothing new and took away time they could have spent on reading or studying. "Gain in knowledge of current events was negligible because children had little interest in these programmes. There was equally little gain in cultural interests." (p. 21)

9) TV apparently does not make children listless or lead to poor concentration or reduced interest at school, and does not harm the children's eyesight or make them more enterprising or anxious to develop new hobbies.

10) And a last, very hopeful, note: More than half of the children said that if they had to do without television, they *would not miss it.*

If you want scientific proof of the influence on children of television, I'm afraid the above is about as scientific as I can get. There is, after all, no empirical way of proving that a child who stabs his playmate, blows up city hall, or

---

[4] For more recent instances of this sort of gain, see "Ghost Teachers on TV," by Rosalyn L. Switzen, *TV Guide,* June 29, 1968.

steals a tramway bus did so because of watching television. No way, that is, unless we could restore him to his babyhood, with all the same influences, except for TV, and then sit back and await the consequences. Now that would be scientific—and impossible. No more can we prove the effectiveness of a doctor's prescription. We can only observe, and generalize, and keep statistical sheets. And we can use our common sense, remembering that there was a similar international unease at the advent of movies, radio, the telephone, and even printed books.

What about television ads for war toys? for guns, bazookas, rockets and rocket launchers, tanks, grenades? There is a swelling current of criticism today directed not only against the advertisements for such toys but against the toys themselves. Do such toys condition boys for war and violence? I doubt it. If toy guns were not on the market, the kids would carve pieces of wood and broomstick handle and fashion their own M-1's and six-shooters, the way we did during the depression. Or they would simply take a stick and imagine it was a rifle. The key word is "imagine." Children live much of their lives in a world of imagination, whether they are playing with miniature Polaris subs made of styrene or mothering Barbie dolls. Both the mothering and the underwater maneuvers are imaginary, unreal, and that should console us. As the British study, published for the Nuffield Foundation, made clear, violence on television does not disturb children or make them imitate it provided it is presented in a stereotyped fashion which accentuates its unreality. Saturday morning cartoons, by this evidence, do little if any hurt to children since of their very nature they are imaginary. I doubt that Popeye's epic confrontations with his bearded foe made yesterday's children go out and punch one another, any more than they made the same children relish spinach. Both the fights and the ravenous gulping of the greens were too unreal to be imitable. The same thing can be said of the adventures in Grimm's fairy tales, which have lately made some writers blanch and work madly to bowdlerize the "savagery" into something more suitable for tender minds.

It is a useless and even harmful effort. Such fairy tales teach children, in a way specially tailored to their imaginations, that terror and injustice stalk this world and lay low even the best of us at times. To take that knowledge away from them would be a tragedy, a foul act of deception, robbing them not only of a knowledge of evil (the wolf) but also of the heroism of those who contend with evil (the three pigs).

Catholic congregations used to recite a prayer at the end of each parish Mass that began, "Hail, Holy Queen," and included the following interesting words: "To thee [Mary] do we pray, to thee do we send up our sighs, mourning and weeping in this valley of tears." What we have there is a frank, grim declaration of the unpleasantness of part of our lives (sickness, disease, poverty, injustice, etc.). What we have there is an adult and religious version of Jack and the beanstalk. The liturgists have robbed us of the prayer after Mass. I hope that the finicky foes of fairy tales are not allowed to rob the children of the beanstalk, for it is a direct means of access to that second most august of all presences, the presence of evil. An ogre lives at the top of the beanstalk; only a fool would deny him to children. For as long as evil is an ogre, or a hungry wolf, or a cruel stepmother, children will grow to understand it without being terrorized by it. Some years ago scientists at the University of Notre Dame conducted a most interesting experiment. They raised a number of white mice, from the moment of birth, in an absolute germ-free atmosphere. When the mice were later exposed to ordinary air, they took sick and died of innocuous germs that didn't phase their more hardy, germ-ridden brothers. Parents, I suppose, would prefer to raise their children in a germ-free environment. I'm afraid such over-protectiveness would be no more beneficial to the tots than it was to the mice. After all, knowledge must begin to take root in the human mind at some time, the sooner the better, even knowledge of evil. Better intellectually than experientially.

War toys, I believe, are much like fairy tales. They educate children to the reality of evil in history, but in a stylized, stereotyped play of the imagination that neither disturbs nor barbarizes the child. It simply interests the child in the world. And interest, just as much as fear, is the beginning of wisdom. The wailing censors of toy guns and of the Brothers Grimm are as simplistic in their view as those strident guardians of fiction who would emasculate the novel in order to redeem it, who view fiction as either epicene (and therefore good) or obscene (and therefore bad).

I have lately seen newsreel photos of children queueing up at police stations in order to turn in their toy guns. It was a pathetic sight to one who, as a boy, took such keen pleasure in mowing down his playmates and, indeed, in being mowed down by them. Everyone had to take his turn at being killed. It was a question of fair play. As any number of children will tell you, it is far more exciting to fall down dead in a properly dramatic fashion than simply to point a stick rifle and shout, "Bang! Bang!" Dying (and rising from the dead) are as much a part of toy-gun play as going Bang!

Responsible parents, when all is said and done, realize that not all television programs are suitable for their children. Rowan and Martin's "Laugh-In" falls in a different classification than Ding Dong School or Walt Disney. Some shows are simply not suitable for children, others are border-line. The parent must assume the onus of censoring what his child watches. I am aware that "censor" is another of those dirty words of the modern libertarian, but in a very real sense parenthood is almost synonymous with censorship. Good parents will censor their child's diet, clothing, time, playmates, and entertainment. Educating children to a sense of values is censorship, for the moment I establish one value as primary, I relegate others to a subordinate and even undesirable status. Christ was notorious for censoring, for cutting certain values out of life and replacing them with others. (I am reminded of the ten commandments.) If the parent does not act as his child's censor, one wonders just who will.

What is needed is a kind of code which will help guide parents in choosing programs for their children, which will help them make TV viewing a rational part of the family life. Such a code does exist. It was issued a few years ago by the International Catholic Association for Radio and Television, with headquarters in Fribourg, Switzerland. Here is a summary of it, with comments of my own:

1) Two hours a day of TV viewing should be the absolute maximum. An hour and a half would be better. If your child wants to watch all day, he (or you) may have a big problem. Consult your physician or psychiatrist—or your priest or minister.

2) Horror programs are taboo. This stipulation jibes with the findings of the Nuffield Foundation study.

3) Children must not get the idea that they have a right to watch any show that mom and dad watch. This rule may at first glance look like hypocrisy of the "do as I say, not as I do" variety. But it isn't. There are worthwhile programs which are suitable for adults but not for children. I suppose this undemocratic view of family life is what led Paul Goodman to say that "the family is the American Fascism." He would prefer, I take it, that program selection in the family be made on the basis of a secret ballot, an eventuality which strikes me as a cogent argument in favor of birth control. And incidentally, if a program is just plain dirty, no one should watch it.

4) TV has no place at meal times.

5) Mom and Dad should agree beforehand on what programs Junior can watch, and not debate the issue in his presence. If they turn off objectionable programs with frank reasons to the child why they did so, the child will learn to make his own responsible choices.

6) Parents and teachers should write letters or cards to television producers and sponsors expressing approval or disapproval. It is surprising what an impact such communications have. Television personnel, like newspapermen and writers in general, sometimes feel as if they were working in an absolute vacuum. They like to know somebody out there is looking in. They want your approval.

7) Parents should require that normal family life and the regular bedtime hour not be upset by the children's viewing hours.

It's easier said than done. Of course, it is. But necessary all the same. The man who writes about the proper training of children before proving his competence at same is risking grave perils. But someone must do it. Objections of this nature always remind me of what a learned Jesuit once said. Somebody had questioned him over the propriety of writing about sanctity before one had actually achieved it. To which the Jesuit replied, "If I wait until I achieve all the virtues before writing about them, I will write only on my coffin lid—the inside of the lid."

Parents are not alone in their anxiety about the effects of television and television commercials on their children. Let me reassure them by citing the Television Code of the National Association of Broadcasters. In section 1 (e) the Code states:

Television broadcasters should exercise the utmost care and discrimination with regard to advertising material, including content, placement and presentation, near or adjacent to programs designed for children. No considerations of expediency should be permitted to impinge upon the vital responsibility toward children and adolescents, which is inherent in television, and which must be recognized and accepted by all advertisers employing television.[5]

Later on, under the title "Acceptability of Advertisers and Products—General," the Code gets more specific, always with the idea in mind that television is a family medium and that there are children in the family. Most of the Code's stipulations are admirable, one or two are inconsistent, and some are amusing. For example, I cannot understand why the advertising of hard liquor and the actual consuming of beer and wine in a commercial are forbidden, when children are permitted to see actors and actresses gulp gallons of the stuff on network dramas, and to listen to one crooner-comedian who apparently, so far as the children are concerned, owes much of his popularity to his (imaginary) capacity to imbibe booze. Under section 1 (f) the Code requires that products "of a personal nature" be treated with special emphasis on ethics and good taste. On June 7, 1956, a special board convened to study this ruling and concluded that products for the treatment of hemorrhoids and for use in connection with feminine hygiene are unacceptable. I wonder if they saw some parity between the two?

The Code also bans the advertising of fortune-telling (does that include fortune cookies?), occultism, spiritualism, astrology, phrenology, palm-reading, numerology, and character reading. Yet mind readers, soothsayers, and other practitioners of e.s.p. and the *psi* factor (Peter Hurkos, Crisswell, Jeanne Dixon, *et al*) turn up time and time again on television talk shows where they bemuse millions of viewers with their goetic charades. (How have they overlooked the black Mass and the reading of chicken entrails?) Since prophets of doom like to compare contemporary

[5] Cited by Arthur Bellaire, *TV Advertising* (New York: Harper & Brothers, 1959), Appendix I, p. 250.

America with ancient Rome in her ponderous decline, I find it interesting to note that the typical Roman, a lover of order, objected to private soothsayers (à la Jeanne Dixon, and the others). Soothsaying was something only the State was competent to do. The Latin verb *hariolor,* which meant "to utter prophecies privately," ended up by meaning "to talk nonsense." I think the time is ripe to revive the word.

There is an old Spanish proverb which goes: *Más sabe el diablo por viejo que por diablo.* The devil knows more from being old than from being the devil. Experience, or tradition if you like, is essential to an ordered civilization. That explains why folklore prefers the old broom, which leaves some dirt behind, to the new one, which whisks everything away indiscriminately. It is understandable that young idealists, being by nature new brooms, would wish to purge our culture of hypocrisy (whether in TV commercials or politics or the operation of mega-universities) by sweeping the whole establishment into the dustbin. The proper response to their criticism does not lie in "getting down to their level," a bad habit, by the way, of so many adult hosts of children's TV shows. It lies rather in reestablishing ourselves as adults more securely in our own level, one, it may be hoped, of reason, knowledge, logic, dignity, and sincerity.

The "getting down to their level" school is enjoying current popularity. David Riesman noted some time back how teachers in a Denver high school imitated the colloquial greeting of the most popular student.[6] (I can't imagine my high school Latin teacher, Stephen Krieger, S.J., ever meeting me in the halls of Regis High with, "Greetings Gates, let's communicate.") The Cincinnati *Post and Times-Star* has reported on one of the "new breed" of levelers, this time a young priest, who came to dinner at the home of a city probation officer, Phil Muldoon, father of three boys,

[6] David Riesman, *The Lonely Crowd* (Garden City: Doubleday, 1950), p. 102.

aged 12, 10, and 8. When he arrived the priest was wearing two lapel pins. One said "Help the Morally Retarded." The other, "Help Bring Back Paganism." When Muldoon asked the young cleric to say grace, he responded as follows: "Rub-a-dub-dub, rub-a-dub-dub, thanks for the grub, yea God!" Muldoon is quoted as saying he was a "bit surprised," but added, "A lot of young fellows today have a tough time identifying with authority, and when a young priest can joke along with them it goes over big." I'm sure it does. Grace before meals has long been ripe for a gag. So have the Mass vestments. Why not put "Help" or "I Dig God" or something groovy like that on them instead of the same old dull crosses or grapes or sheaves of wheat?

What I am going to say about "identifying with authority" is very useful to advertisers who are trying to get the young to "identify" with their products, preferably from the time they begin to wear rompers. The question is: how can you get youth to identify with authority? Answer: you can't. No youngster will ever be able to identify with authority for the reason that he is not a part of it. Authority is not his bag. "Author" and "authority" obviously have the same derivation, namely, an originator, a creator, the founder of a family, none of which concepts is closely identified with childhood or youth. There can be no identification between unlike things. The Romantics thought otherwise. They believed man could identify with the holm oak, the bush tit, the kinkajou monkey, the pie-eyed daisy, and other animal and vegetable forms. Geoffroy Saint-Hilaire once remarked that while lying on the banks of the Nile he felt the instincts of the crocodile awakening in his soul. More recently Sally Carrighar wrote an entire article on how to make friends with animals. "Sparrows and mice are well worth knowing for their own sakes." [7] Whether they are

---

[7] Sally Carrighar, "How to Make Friends With Animals," *Saturday Evening Post*, March 12, 1955, p. 115.

or not, Miss Carrighar does have one recommendation that advertisers might well heed. In talking to animals, she advises, never, but never, use baby talk. It repels them because it's artificial. If you want to establish communication with a squirrel or chipmunk, just say what you're thinking. To a chipmunk she said, "Sometimes you whirl so fast, you are just a brown blur." That couldn't help but win the chipmunk over. When we are communicating with children, we might well follow the same rule: be adult and genuine. If it worked with a woodland mouse, it can work with children.

The only other solution to this "identification with authority" crisis that has worked us into such a tizzy is to put children in places of authority, a goal which some of them are trying to realize at this very moment. It is an entirely unacceptable remedy, unless one accepts the Romantic view of the child as an "archetypal holy innocent," full of pure wisdom and genius, as Wordsworth and Rosseau did, as Allen Funt does.

I prefer to believe that children are learners who, in the fulness of time, and then only, having acquired some measure of maturity and experience, should be given their own opportunity to botch things up. And I am convinced, further, that they are influenced least by adults who try to get down to their level in hip lingo, mod clothing styles, or whatever. Writers of children's TV shows and commercials will have little lasting influence on the young if they continue their condescending "Hi there, kiddies" approach. That goes double for theologians. What children want from adults, and they make no bones about it, is honesty. And it is just not honest for an adult to ape the mannerisms and habits of children. Children are natural mimics (one reason why languages should be taught in the earliest grades) ; how can we expect them to mimic adult behavior if we stuff our advertising and our theology with juvenilia?

I had thought of writing an entire chapter on Vance Packard's concept of the "psychoseduction" of children by television advertisers. But it seems a futile undertaking. In the long run, children will buy whatever their parents allow them to buy. If our advertisers exploit the kiddies, if they send the little ones on an epidemic wave of piggie-bank smashing, it is the parents' fault for not training their dear little moppets in the rational use of money.

Whenever the question of children and their proper formation comes up, my mind is haunted by an incident that occurred some years ago. It concerns the late Father Dan Lord, S.J., who devoted a lifetime to writing and speaking to children and youth about Christ and His good word. Not long before he died, Father Lord was talking with a friend of mine, a Jesuit who taught me in college. My friend praised Father Lord for his great work with adolescents but the latter only sighed and said, "You know, I spent my life talking to the wrong people. I should have been talking to the parents." I think that all advertising men, whether they work for a corporate body in advertising or the Mystical Body of Christ in propagating Christian doctrine, should take Father Lord's words to heart. They had better address the parents, but in a language that children can assimilate and enjoy.

The Bible, according to the science of hermeneutics, is the most consciously written book in the history of man. Nothing was *put into* it without a definite reason. I would go further and say, nothing was *left out* without a definite reason. One of the things omitted is a talk by our Lord to children. He talks *about* them, never *to* them. Why? Because He knew that the parents (adults) matter first. Our romantic and sentimental adulation of childhood has blinded us to that great truth. The parents matter most. They are the ones who form the child, who fill his clutching mind and heart with ideals, hopes, love, faith, virtue. Or else they give him nothing but food, clothes, and money—that is, they give him nothing. Father Lord's awakening was to this reality. To influence children, you must turn to the parents. They, not children, are the hope of the nation. Where will we find "love abounding in knowledge"? In parents. I really think we are wasting time maundering over TV's influence on the kids. We should rather be asking: How does TV influence the parents? Violence and the adolescent —nonsense. Rather, how does violence affect the parents? And pornography? And illicit sex in films and books? What do they do to the ideals of parents? If parents are helped to achieve a full Christian life, the problem of adolescent delinquency will resolve itself. I'm not saying that all one has to do is educate parents and motivate them to take their responsibilities seriously and, presto, all our troubles are over and teenage "rebellion" is at an end. Things are not that simple! But I am saying that concentrated efforts in adult education, in helping parents to mature, to show their children by their lives what responsible, mature living means will do a lot to alleviate the problems facing our society today.

By a curious coincidence, two of the most popular novels of recent times among juveniles and collegians both deal with this question: What is a child? One of them, Salinger's *Catcher in the Rye,* answers: A child is an unsullied creature whose nature is spoilt by adult stupidity and selfishness. The only truly admirable character in the entire book is Holden Caulfield's little sister. The other book, William Golding's *Lord of the Flies,* answers in a different strain: A child is a young creature whose nature bears the scars of some ancient evil. The children in this work, free from adult influence on their remote island, establish a kind of juvenile state. It is characterized by the same panoply of virtues and vices one would find in an adult society. Salinger's view is sentimental, Romantic; Golding's, traditional, realist, Christian.

It's rather discouraging to reflect that we are trying to form (or reform) children without being able to agree on what precisely they are. One could do worse than follow Christ's lead. He said: "Let the little children come unto me." *That* was said to parents and adults. Do you think He knows something we don't? Like, it is the parents who determine just where their children go: to Christ, or to— well, what are the alternatives?

I think mother and dad had better put their foot down, and soon. For no one can exercise stable authority while standing on one leg.

CHAPTER 9

Hi There, Fund-Seekers!

A home for wayward boys on the Pacific Coast was in grave danger a few years ago of going out of business. It had few boys, fewer funds, and was about to lose its status as an agency of the state's juvenile authority, thanks in large part to gross mismanagement at all levels. Then a dynamic young director was appointed. As one of his first moves, he launched a nationwide direct-mail appeal for funds, enclosing snappy literature about the home, and giving it a new name and new "image," that smacked of "Jimmy-Cagney-Pat-O'Brien-Win-one-for-the-Gipper." The results were staggering. Money poured in by the millions of dollars. So engulfing was this monsoon of dollars that a local post office employee, concluding there was plenty of cash to go around, helped himself and was promptly arrested. And even as I write, an assistant director is under investigation by the Bureau of Internal Revenue.

Every organization in the land in need of money (is there one that isn't?) knows the value of appeals by direct mail. The blizzard of envelopes containing such appeals bulges postmen's mailbags, drifts higher and higher in our mailboxes, and at any moment may bury the Post Office Department altogether. But such appeals require names and addresses. As a result, any organization is willing to trade (or sell) its mailing list to others so as to expand its list of potential victims. The traffic in mailing lists alone by these insatiable fundseekers is positively breathtaking. I suppose if one enjoys getting mail, any mail, he will rejoice over all this third-class garbage in his mail slot. If not, he can—what can he do?

A number of Catholic organizations have added a new dimension to their direct-mail pleas for cash. They are enclosing in their appeals some sort of cheap gimcrack, usually with a vaguely religious motif, calling it a "gift" in their pitch, and then asking for a "donation." The idea is to make the recipient feel guilty about keeping the item, guilty enough to send off a few centavos in the return mail. It works. My God, how it works!

One should begin by admitting that most (but not all) of the uses to which the money will be put are good ones. We would like to help the children of Missionhurst, to build cooperative silos in Guatemala, or schools in the Congo and the Philippines, and shelters for the refugees in Hong Kong. The Indians in the Pallottine Father's Brazilian missions need and deserve education, food, vitamins, and medicine, and money to keep their hospital in the Mato Grosso functioning. We are all appalled by that photograph of the old Indian's ulcerated and leprous hands, by the 4-year-old girl who must eat dirt to satisfy her stomach worms. We want to help them. We long to help train Marianist priests, to assist the homeless and wounded in Bishop Paul Seitz's Kontum diocese in South Vietnam. We want to help Rev. Father Ralph, Drawer X, Boys Town, the Society for the Propagation of the Faith, the Red Cross, the United Fund, and the Cerebral Palsy drive. We'd like to further research into leukemia, arthritis, Brights' disease, cystic fibrosis, muscular dystrophy, cancer, and heart disease. And what about the Boy and Girl Scouts,

Campfire Girls, Boys Clubs, Teen Canteens, Blind Veterans, etc.?

I said earlier that the money from these appeals was put to good uses "for the most part." What made me qualify that statement was the literature emanating from St. Jude's Shrine in Baltimore. I'm not so sure that I want to help promote devotion to "the saint of the impossible." Not that I doubt the efficacy of prayer to Jude. He may very well have cured Mrs. A.D.'s husband after he suffered his sub-achrinoid stroke, preserved Mrs. A.L.'s leg from amputation, and arranged that Mrs. J.S.'s tumor and marriage both be benign. But are devotions to saints "promoted" by injections of cash like this? What possible benefit can anyone derive from buying a votive light which will "burn perpetually before the statue of St. Jude at this Center of St. Jude's Devotions"? The cost of that "perpetual" light, by the way, is $1 per week. So the light will not be perpetual unless you keep that $1 per week coming in, folks. In what sense is that candle a prayer? In what sense is it Christian? Candles, as every pastor will admit deep in his heart, are a gimmick to raise cash. Period.

Unfortunately Father Luciani (initials P.U.), director of this St. Jude shrine, is a relentless mailer of appeals. Last spring he enclosed some Easter cards to make us feel guilty, cards "which you can send to your friends. . . . Of course the Easter cards are not for sale. We can only accept donations." How's that? Oh, it's something to do with Federal statutes, income tax, that sort of thing. Not with religion. He goes on: "When you send the Easter cards to your friends, please be sure to send me their names so that they can share in spiritual benefits promised on each card." Though he doesn't explicitly say so, I'm sure Father Luciani would also appreciate it if you would send along your friends' addresses too. Eureka! a mailing list, and at no extra cost to him.

Father Luciani also mails out "free" ballpoint pens, in Marian blue, with "St. Jude Shrine" inked on in sedate black, together with the invocation, "St. Jude—Pray for Us." Yes, do, St. Jude! Pray for us! And above all, pray that our faith will survive these assaults on it by pious *colporteurs* of plastic statues, medals and chains, thermometers encapsulated in plastic fish (oh see the symbolism), rosaries, cards for every occasion under the sun (except Guy Fawkes day), key holders and key chains, miniature Indian totem poles and tom-tom mallets from Montana and South Dakota, plastic holy water fonts, note pads, letter openers, tiny wall plaques, shrines, pictures of St. Anthony, jewelry, address-labels for envelopes, plastic automobile crucifixes all dressed up in gilt and "blessed for you by the Missionhurst Fathers," and even raffle tickets. Yes, St. Jude, by all means pray for us.

All the above knickknacks, purchased in gross lots for a few pennies each, are expected by the religious promoters to bring in "donations" of $1 and up. They are mailed unsolicited to the address of any Catholic the promoters can lay their hands on. They offer, in addition, other, more expensive items, too dear to be shipped without cash on the barrel head, and veritably smacking of piety: a hostess electric bun warmer ($15 "or more"), electric tray, "peelerparer miracle worker," a dandy all-purpose vegetable knife that can be used either left or right-handed and that peels apples, pares potatoes, and shreds cabbage, all the while reminding the user of the sacred mystery of miracles; regency geranium nugget to hold "the happy flower," flower arranger, fruit bowl, carving sets, steak knives, "spiritual alliance cards" by the boxful, first-aid kits, tissue dispensers, can openers, ceramic salt and pepper shakers (with "inspiring prayer"), and even a diamond glow aurora borealis pendant of the praying hands in a gift box with 24-carat gold chain ($3 "or more").

The least incendiary remark one can make about this priming of the pumps (from which charity floweth not) is to call it automated mendicancy. It is the religious stepchild of our mechanized age, an age redolent of computers and automation—and its retinue of men in white coats. The Church must trim her sails (as she always has) to take into account the prevailing winds and tides of each generation. Though we may flinch at the thought of Cardinals and bishops marking punch-card ballots at a synod in Rome, there is something to be said for it. It beats raising the hand or shouting "Non placet." And priests can reach far more of the people in Fords and Chevvies and Ramblers than in dogcarts or Wells-Fargo stagecoaches. The bucolic Church of our forefathers, whether we like it or not, must and has become the banausic Church of the 20th century.[1]

But one wonders just how many workshop techniques can be introduced into religion without changing Christ's Mystical Body into some sort of monstrous, cybernated robot, programmed by IBM instead of I.H.S. The vision of an automated Church inspired Malcolm Muggeridge to say recently of America, "Religion is little more than an efficiently run business enterprise. I actually heard one clergyman refer to his church as 'my plant.'"[2] Only one! I've seldom heard anything else.

"For the love of Christ," Bishop Sheen once exhorted a group of priests, "stop being administrators and start being shepherds of souls!" And we may amend that to, "Stop being marketing analysts."

If there is a single sentiment which is characteristic of those today who cry most loudly for reformation of Church and State, it is a repugnance for the mass of the people

[1] At the 1968 Southern California Exposition in Del Mar, large signs above the booth of the Wright Bible Distributors of Hawaiian Gardens, Calif., announced, "World's Automatic Bible." And a project called Thabor offers conferences to the clergy "on tape and LP records."

[2] The Denver *Post*, May 12, 1968.

(i.e., the middle class). I don't know why this should be so, but it seems inevitable. In the first century before Christ, when the poet Horace deigned to present his own plan for the salvation of the Roman State in six odes, his very first line was: *Odi profanum vulgus et arceo* (Lib. III, Carm. I). It may be loosely translated, "I despise the common rabble, and I want nothing to do with them." Not a very noble sentiment for a savior. But then I've noticed that saviors (with one notable exception) are not long on compassion. Many of our Catholic "saviors" are refusing nowadays to even worship with the rest of us and have gone "underground."

Perhaps their recognition of our wretched plight, which drove them into saviorhood in the first place, is so vivid it turns their stomachs and forces them to redeem us from afar. If the Church had never uttered a word about the divinity of Christ, this one fact alone would almost prove that He is God: He knows all about us, and He loves us anyway!

But our other saviors! Edward R. F. Sheehan, from somewhere just to the right of the Thrones and Dominations, looks down at us 50 million American Catholics and sounds the eighth trumpet: "True, most of the laity are still apathetic." [3] What an extraordinary canvassing job that must have been. And carried out so quickly. Surely Mr. Sheehan would be immensely useful to Dr. Gallup, or to the Nielsen TV rating system, and especially to political candidates wondering how they stand with the electorate. And how cannily the liturgists scan our incorporate faces while we millions are at worship and tell, from the cast of our eye or the way we flip a page or click a bead, that our participation is "sadly wanting in depth and understanding." It's positively phrenological. "The Church in America," declares

[3] Edward R. F. Sheehan, "Not Peace but the Sword," *Look*, Nov. 28, 1964, p. 42.

Father Justin Sorrel, O.C.D., "is the largest group of 'white racists' in the world." I can't help feeling that Father Sorrel was assisted in his canvass by Mr. Sheehan. And John L. McKenzie, S.J.: "The statement [that America is a Christian country] is so manifestly false that one does not know how to frame the denial."[4] And Dan Herr: "The bigots [the Catholic kind, he means] are on every side of us."[5] So soon have we forgotten John XXIII (so soon forgotten his efforts to enlighten the prophets of doom, so soon forgotten his openness of mind and heart. Alas, Postumus, the fleeting years do indeed slip by.

But what has this distaste for us by our new saviors got to do with the religious mailing racket? It isn't the Catholic people, after all, who are putting this junk into the mails; it's a few zealous entrepreneurs who have confused the American Business Creed with that of Athanasius. The point is, only a people of heroic patience and extraordinary faith would have submitted to this begging racket without either storming the barricades at St. Jude's Shrine in Baltimore (or at the other shrines of junk mail), or else giving up the faith altogether. The Catholic people did neither. Rather they gave, and gave—and give. The pandemic state of the junk mail racket today is a monument to their eleemosynary generosity.

I have never seen an estimate of how many pieces of alms-mail are posted every year. Such a statistic might be, in Daniel Seligman's terminology, either unknowable or meaningless, or both. But since even the devil cites statistics to his comfort, let me make a stab at it. I have ample precedent. Dr. J. Douglas McCluskie of the Denver Public Health Department reported in 1963 that Denver rats had "a flea index" of 0.12 per rat. Quite a good showing. A recent ad reported that over 48 million Americans

---

[4] "Q.E.D.," a column in *The Critic*, April-May, 1968, p. 11.
[5] "Stop Pushing," *ibid.*, p. 6.

wear dentures. Dr. Joyce Brothers has assured us that the average American girl kisses 79 men before marriage. And there is enough energy in a ton of coal to—to drive a space vehicle clear to—well, way out there. So here goes. I would "guesstimate" that the pieces of junk religious mail shipped off each year number well up in the hundreds of millions. All of my Catholic friends (and some of my non-Catholic ones) receive such items, many of them once or twice a week. An illustration will show the reasonableness of this statistic. In September of 1968 an executive in Milwaukee was approached by a man who wished to rent an addresso-graph machine. Why? Because a nun from an Indian mission was sending out a letter appealing for $10,000 with which to operate the mission school. I said "a letter." In fact, she was mailing over *five million* copies of that appeal at a cost of $50,000. The pitch in her letter was to her poverty and her need to raise $10,000!

The Mission Secretariat, composed of all the mission-sending societies in the United States, both men and women, recognizes the need for some sort of unified fund-collecting operation. The problem of junk mail was raised by a speaker at the Secretariat's 1967 meeting, though nothing came of it. The monies collected by these mission societies annually were pegged during that meeting at around $41 million, this in addition to the $16 million collected by the Society for the Propagation of the Faith. Not all of the Catholic junk mail practitioners (e.g., the Shrine of St. Jude in Baltimore) belong to the Secretariat, and not all of the $41 million is the result of junk mail. But the sum helps us appreciate the grotesque amplitude of this religious racket.

I can do no better than echo the advice given not long ago by the National Information Bureau in New York City with regard to the countless appeals made for funds. Said the Bureau: if you get any unordered item through the mails, pay no attention to it. Neither reply to the appeal nor return the article. This method of fund-raising, NIB reports, can cost as much as 90 cents of every dollar contributed.

I have just received in the mails from Rev. Father Ralph (does he really exist?) a box of Christmas cards with the usual request for "an offering in appreciation for the Christmas cards." I do not appreciate the cards and shall send in no offering, following the advice of the NIB. But what worries me is the card which I am asked to return to the S.V.D. Catholic Universities in Chicago, along with my offering. It is a punched address card, all ready for the computer, and printed at the bottom of it is this unlikely combination of sentences: "Please do not tear, tape or fold. Use of this card provides more for God's work." The use of such a card would point to the magnitude of the junk mail racket. It does not point to God.

I wish I had Mr. Sheehan's uncanny canvassing powers so that I could have made the junk mail statistic more accurate. But at least its terms are meaningful. One can define third-class mail with a piece of "free" merchandise stuck inside and can determine if it originated from a religious source. But how does Mr. Sheehan define "apathetic"? Apathetic to what? What is one man's apathy is another man's patience. One could conceivably compute the postage costs per annum of these direct-mail mendicants, but how on earth does Dan Callahan know that millions of Catholics who go often to Mass and the sacraments do not love their neighbor and that millions of non-Christians manage both to love their neighbor and serve the world? (The wording of that invidious comparison betrays its emotional origin.) What does it mean "to love one's neighbor"? Early Muslim fanatics felt they were doing a good turn to their Christian neighbor by chopping off his head. Francis Xavier at times expressed his compulsive and heroic love of the neighbor by kissing the suppurating sores of the sick. (To his credit, he never imposed that practice on others.) True love of God, from which alone true love of neighbor springs, is measurable only by God and can find expression in an infinite variety of forms, some of which might be acceptable to Mr. Callahan. As for the phrase "serving the world," I leave it to your ingenuity to figure out what that might mean.

In this connection it is worth while to spend some time in commenting on Dan Herr's address to the 58th national convention of the Catholic Press Association in Columbus, Ohio, delivered May 15, 1968. Despite the good intentions motivating his remarks and despite the truth that there is great injustice to the Negro and racism on the part of some white people, Mr. Herr's statement is not logical or fully true. Mr. Herr declared, "But not only does the white American refuse to give his black brother justice, he rejects him, he scorns him, he hates him. And the Catholic no less than, perhaps more than, the non-Catholic." [6]

Just how did Mr. Herr arrive at this murky conclusion? Such a ghastly charge against "American Catholics" must be based on sound supportive evidence. Well, he first mentions those Chicago suburbanites who threw eggs at and otherwise cuffed Negro children who were bussed to schools in white neighborhoods. He does not say how many were guilty of such misdeeds, nor does he know how many of those were Catholics. Let us put the figure at 100. Then he mentions the "virulent campaigns" (he does not say how many) against a recent catechetical textbook series. Assuming, as he does, that this opposition is the fruit of bigotry and not of theological differences (an assumption he makes no effort to prove), let us say that there are five such campaigns and put 10 people in each (a generous figure). Next he

[6] *The Critic,* June-July, 1968, p. 2.

remarks that "in many parishes" buttons are dropped instead of money into the collection baskets to protest "the mildest kind of sermon on brotherhood." We are not told in how many parishes nor given the number of buttons. Let us guess that 20 buttons were dropped in ten parishes, half of them by bigots.

And then there are those horrible "Cody Must Go" bumper stickers. I haven't been in Chicago since primary flight training at Glenview N.A.S., so I can't say how many stickers there are. Perhaps there are 1,000. We shall subtract 500 to exclude the Catholics who are unhappy with poor Cody on other than racial grounds. Next Herr says that of 10,000 letters sent to the mayor of Chicago in regard to his "shoot to kill arsonists" statement, the pro's were 15 to 1 over the anti's. How many of the letters were mailed by Catholics? No one knows. How many were inspired by bigotry? No one can say. (I would have supported the mayor in his stand. As it happens, I live directly above a liquor store operated by whites in a Negro neighborhood. If some firebrand should take it into his noggin to pitch a molotov cocktail among the shelves of Kamchatka and Wolfschmidt, the resultant fire would consume all my books [stacked in shelves and boxes in my closet], over twenty years of filed research material, four manuscripts that are looking for publishers, my typewriter, my clothes, and quite possibly me. Am I a bigot if I prefer that a policeman shoot that individual before he wings his missile through the window and incinerates much and maybe all of my life?)

But let us say that of the 10,000 letters Mayor Daley received, 7,000 were mailed by Catholics and that 500 of these were bigots. Nor must we forget the one nun who "added her inimitable racist comments" to a letter to Herr. I don't know what her letter proves. I heard of a nun who sent a mash-note to the bagboy in a supermarket. It only goes to show that nuns and bagboys are human, but it says little about "the American Catholic."

What are we left with? There are 100 egg throwers, 50 catechism opposers, 100 button droppers, 500 bumper stickers, 500 anti-arsonists, and one nun. Total = 1,251 bigots. There are 50 million Catholics in America. On such evidence Herr concludes, "This is the doomsday issue." I agree wholeheartedly that the racial problem (not only in America but everywhere) is a critical one, but it will not be solved by men who calumniously brand the American Church with the scarlet (rather white) letter B for bigotry.

In his book *True Humanism* (chapter IV) Jacques Maritain makes a valuable distinction between the ideal states or utopias of such men as St. Thomas More, Fenelon, Fourier, and Saint-Simon and his own "historical ideal." Their ideal state, he says, was an unrealizable one. They wrote about a form of government in society which represented the absolute maximum in virtue and sagacity, something therefore that could exist only in their minds (an *ens rationis*) and nowhere else. Maritain, on the other hand, in presenting his own view of the ideal Christian state, has in mind a realizable ideal, a state which could possibly exist in the real world, though in a state of process, or realization.

Writers on spirituality fall into the same two categories. There are those who present as our ideal of virtue the absolute maximum, for example, a totally selfless love of God, with absolutely no thought of reward. They are writing about a spiritual utopia, consummately realized, but able to exist only in their minds and certainly never realizable by any human being, canonized saint or no.

Such a picture, holding out as ideal an unattainable state, can't help but frustrate the reader. He is told, "Here is what you must become." But as he reads, he realizes he can never achieve such a perfect state. The result is that he feels frustrated, perhaps even bitter at a "system" that demands the impossible.

Hagiographers are guilty of a similar error at times. They present the subject of their research as a kind of walking *ens rationis,* clothed in the flesh of their own purple prose. Such a "utopiazation" of the saints will only mislead and aggravate the reader. In my own experience, the commonest complaint made by high school boys in reporting on lives of the saints they have read is: The saint is too perfect. One student, after reading a life of Francis of Assisi, remarked that while Francis as a youth went out on the town and "lived it up a little, he didn't seem ever to have gotten drunk or done anything really wrong." The student was disappointed, not that the saint hadn't sinned seriously (or so he was presented in the book), but that the saint had nothing in common with him. Hagiography like that is false; the saints, at least in their formative years, had everything in common with us.

Critics of the Church had better keep Maritain's distinction in mind when they assess the state of affairs in America. Otherwise they will lose their perspective. Tunnel vision is just as unacceptable in scholarship as it is in pilot training. Perhaps the grander one's goals, the more inflamed his rhetoric is likely to be. The man who insists on the instant fulfillment of all the possibilities latent in the mustard seed may necessarily erupt in lyrical crescendoes of prose golliwoggery, and to hell with reason and logic.

My own aims are more modest. I wish that the cataract of junk mail would dry up, and the sooner the better. Let Father Luciani and his huckstering brethren quit sending their letter openers out into the harvest to do their reaping for them. Catholic fund-raising agencies of all sorts would quickly adopt a unified approach to their work if Catholics simply stopped responding to these cheap appeals. I would recommend that the whole concept of sending donations by mail be seriously evaluated and overhauled. A priest who spent all of 1967 in active work for his mission society told me recently that the theft of such donations by some Post Office employees is scandalous. "They are pros," he remarked, "and they know where to look and what to take. One noted missionary society loses donations by the sackful." Of course Post Office inspectors attempt to catch the culprits, but the area is large and the money-stuffed envelopes are too numerous for such detective work to be 100% effective. You can begin to appreciate the problems involved when you reflect on the fact that one small missionary society in South America is given some $500,000 per year, usually in small donations of $1 or $5, from the Catholics in *one* large eastern diocese. How much never gets past the professional thieves is anybody's guess.

The Church will survive without the tom-toms and key chains shipped off at the drop of a mailing list. Missionaries need not fear that they would be left unaided. American Catholics would not let them down. A University of Michigan study made in 1961 revealed that Americans give over 17 billion a year to churches, charity, and the needy, an average of $300 per family. Moreover, the Catholic school system (for which I have the highest respect) depends almost completely on the open-handed generosity of the derided and scorned American Catholic. It is not the charity of the Catholic citizen that is in need of resuscitation; it is the techniques for begging in use by various church groups. Financial frankness in the Church has become a commonplace among editorial writers today. Dioceses are starting to publish accounts of their budgets and allocation of resources. Parish laymen are asking for, and getting, a share in the disbursement of parish funds (their money, by the way), or at least an explanation of how it is being spent. And not too soon. Frankness is just as necessary in a discussion of the junk mailing racket by religious societies. We may say first of all that it is just that, a racket, an organized, scientifically conducted rape of the American Catholic pocket book, a computerized toying with the guilt feelings of a big-hearted people who apparently find it next to impossible to turn down any appeal to their charity. It is, in addition, a source of intense interest on the part of the Internal Revenue Service. As a service to the Church, may I suggest that Father Ralph and the others publish at the end of the year a complete list of the donations they have received, with an indication of just how much of this money went to their spiritual work and how much to the costs of a staff to mail out all the appeals. It might be an eye-opening account. Until such accounts are published, those who "fall for" such appeals by mail might well be classified as "suckers."

It takes a certain amount of humility to admit it, but the fact is we can't do everything, we can't help everyone, we can't give money to every cause. Unlike God Almighty, whose bag of riches has no bottom, we must establish priorities. And that, it seems to me, is something each individual man must do in the privacy of his conscience, free from the hectoring of self-appointed heads of Holy War Production Boards who feel constrained to tell us all just how to love God, or who rather tell us that we must all love God in one way—their way.

Catholics for the most part know that highest on their list of priorities come their own family (its present and future needs) and their own parish church, where every day the thing Christ did on the cross is prolonged, extended, shattering space and time, no longer His sacrifice but His-and-ours, enriching us beyond belief. The *illuminati* in these parlous days may find it chic to deplore church buildings as wastes of money (they *do* keep out the wind and the rain), and even to question the worthwhileness of the Mass itself. They might as well scold Jesus for wasting himself on the cross at Calvary when he could have been heading up a *matzos* or *kreplach* kitchen in the slums of Jerusalem.

CHAPTER 10

Connoisseurs of Compost

The rich body of Jewish folk-literature contains a series of droll stories about the so-called "fools of Chelm." Chelm is a real town in Poland which emerged in folklore as a kind of breeding ground of innocent stupidity. It is like Gotham in England, or Schildburg in Germany, or Burriana in Spain. I can't think of an American equivalent, though Jack Benny used to break up audiences by mentioning Cucamonga and Pismo Beach. And I have it on the highest authority that on the Atlantic Seaboard, if you mention you are from Wheeling or Ogallala or Pottstown (or anywhere from that continental middleground known as "the sticks"), you are sure to provoke at least a smile.

One of the "fools of Chelm" stories, at any rate, concerns an old man who has been riding for hours on a hot, dusty train without any water. A stranger seated opposite him grows more and more restive as the old fellow repeats over and over again, "Oy, do I have thirst! Oy, am I thirsty!" When the train finally stops at a station, the stranger bolts from the car, returns with a cup of water for the old man, and settles back in his seat for what he hopes will be a more pleasant journey. But in a moment the silence is broken. "Oy," glooms the old man, "did I have a terrible thirst!"

Now make a few substitutions. Put the old man in his bathroom shaving and repeating, "Oh, what a terrible shave!" Have his wife give him a new razor blade. Then, as he mows down the whiskers, have him murmur gloomily, "Oh, what a wonderful shave!" Yes, it's that recent TV commercial for thin Gillettes. (Or is it Schick stainless?) To their credit, ad writers are ransacking the whole library of knowledge in their search for material that will improve their commercials, even stories of the fools of Chelm.

They quote Buddha: "Though one should in battle conquer a thousand men a thousand times, he who conquers himself has the more glorious victory." They reproduce art of all ages, from the splashy abstractions of the former Sister Corita to the melancholy pieties of Fra Angelico. They pore over history, literature, science, classical mythology, and even fairy tales. (Doesn't Little Red Riding Hood's wolf use Bactine?)

The result is to make advertising more original, more interesting, and above all more pedagogical. It is being given a fuller, more complex message than the simple admonition, "Buy." It teaches a system of values, attitudes toward people and things. And through the use of mini-dramas in which the sponsor's message is acted out, it teaches lessons about family life, human relationships, and what other people think and do (and therefore prize). It is a kind of literature (or art form) unto itself, and it is as spirited, as deadly earnest, and as tendentious as the prophet Isaias shouting "Woe upon the Assyrian!" It should be examined, then, on two grounds: 1) How well is it getting its message across? 2) What is the substance of the message?

Many people, and all advertising agencies, feel that advertising gets its message across. They cite the amounts of money spent on advertised items to prove their case. There is, however, no conclusive evidence that the amount of money Americans spend for things would decrease if advertising were suddenly to be eliminated. What advertising certainly does influence is the direction of our spending. Even without advertising, we would still spend $9 billion a year on liquor, though probably not on the same brands.

But there can be no doubt that Americans spend lots of money. We consume more than 12 billion aspirin tablets a year, puff upwards of 475 billion cigarettes at a cost of over $6.5 billion. We are called a children of prodigal living habits who have been lured off our ship of destiny by the siren song of advertising and are now on the beach, wallowing like pigs in the ordure of our luxury. And whose fault is it? Advertising's.

Critics often certify our depravity by citing statistics on alcoholism. The statistics, like many others, are disputed of course. The National Council of Alcoholism reports that 3% of wage earners are alcoholics whose drinking costs industry a billion dollars a year in lost man-hours. The president of the Licensed Beverage Industries supplied different figures: ½ of 1% of wage earners who cost industry one-sixth of the NCA figure. In either case, the statistics are depressing. What are we to make of them?

For perspective, we should note that alcoholism, like the race problem, is not limited to the United States. The French government's Information Committee reported in 1960 that the country spent one tenth of its revenue on drinking and curing the effects of drinking. The relative cost, according to the committee, was twice as high as in Italy, three times higher than in England and Sweden, and five times higher than in America. Those who insist on crying out, "America is doomed!" should logically include many other major nations of the world in their apocalyptic pronouncements. The rest of us, while deploring the damage done by excessive drinking, can profitably reflect that two million Americans are not an entire nation.

Statistics, moreover, can be dreadfully misleading. Some years ago, for instance, a survey reported that one-third of the coeds at Johns Hopkins University married faculty members. A truly amazing statistic—until one learns that at the time of the survey Johns Hopkins had only three women students. We must similarly be on our guard when we read that "the average American family" spends so many dollars per year on alcohol. The statement should more accurately be rendered, "The amount spent yearly by American families on alcohol averages out at so much per family." Those who entertain at lavish cocktail parties several times per week not only raise the "average consumption" of the teetotaling and abstemious families but prove the assertion that there is no such thing as an average family —except mathematically. If an elephant should gain access to a water hole frequented only by a flock of sparrows, a statistician might calculate the number of gallons of water consumed there annually and report, "The average sparrow drinks so many gallons of water per year." In fact, such an "average sparrow" does not exist. To make the analogy absolutely plain, the alcoholics and other "social drinkers" in the United States are the elephants in the water hole, and they have made statisticians painfully exaggerate the liquor capacity of the majority of us sparrows.

A collision has occurred in our country between a great mass of people and an unprecedented amount of buying power. The shock of this collision has generated massive statistics. Now these statistics should make us all ponder deeply the values which are operative in our lives, but they do not condemn a whole people to cultural depravity. Someone wails that Americans are travel-mad since they drive their cars more than 935 billion miles per year. That is less than 10,000 miles per vehicle, by the way, no sure sign we have utterly abandoned God in favor of the open road. In California one can drive 50 miles just to go to church. And there are the 45 million tickets to the movies we buy each week, the $2.5 billion on boating per year, $1 billion on bowling, $1 billion on hunting, $800 million on golf, $150 million on dancing lessons, and $2.6 million on fishing. And while we were at it, we puffed a total of 7.2 million cigars. The total for recreation comes to $40 billion a year.

Before you lift your eyes in horror toward heaven, remember that the recreational spending amounts to about $215 per family, or $85 less than the family gives to charity. And remember too that a father and mother have a duty, repeat *duty,* to provide a certain amount of recreation for themselves and their children. So while some of the $40 billion may represent a pagan excess, not all of it does by a long shot. Still not convinced? Then keep in mind that the government spends billions of tax dollars every year on all sorts of humane and charitable and philanthropic causes, not only in the United States but all over the world. (The Peter's Pence collection, incidentally, which is taken up each year among American Catholics, provides the Pope with most of the monetary assistance that he gets for various charitable and educational works. This information was given me by a member of a religious order and scholar who asked that his name not be used.) The American's tax bill is assuredly a part of his religious tithe, as the Jewish people recognized their taxes to be centuries ago. Yet Bill Moyers, an ex-presidential press secretary, gets up before a nationwide TV audience on ABC and tells the American people that we have not lost our virtue; we never had any in the first place (July 4, 1968)! I wish someone would stand up and tell him that he is full of applesauce.

We spend billions of dollars a year on all sorts of things, true. Advertising has stimulated this spending, true. There is crime and corruption among some of our people, true. (We didn't invent them. Maybe the Russians did.) Therefore, argue the prophets of doom, we are a spiritually bankrupt people. Rubbish!

America is huge, her virtues and vices are huge. But she has a largeness of spirit which astonishes and captivates visitors. "This is the land of all the generosities," Father Brodrick, noted English Jesuit historian and biographer, wrote me not long before his death. "And I have fallen deeply in love with it." "The United States," wrote Andre Maurois, "is a friendly, generous country with real equality among its people. . . the Marshall Plan was generous, efficacious, and disinterested." [1]

In every age there exist men who specialize in spiritual brinkmanship, who spend their lives picking at intellectual manure heaps, much as the early Baja California Indians used to pluck undigested seeds out of their own excrement for further nourishment. These connoisseurs of compost flirting with the precipice of despair tell us we lack a historical sense. These cognoscenti of midden accuse us of having but a captious acquaintance with Hegelianism, and say we are victims of medievalism, or materialism (would a materialist give so much money away?), or violence. Their theme is: "God and honor are dead." The truth is: "The Lord is near." A poor ex-fisherman wrote the latter, and so far as I know he had never heard of the Ivy League.

Let's agree, at any rate, that advertising is getting its message across. Just what is that message? Does it "avoid all elements of corruption and promote Christian values?" Those are the goals Pius XII laid down for radio and television in his address to the Second World Congress for the Lay Apostolate (Oct. 5, 1957). How close does contemporary advertising come to that ideal? One of the criticisms most often leveled at advertising, on television at any rate, is that it irritates by reason of its decibels, its repetitiveness,

---

[1] André Maurois, "Why Europeans Criticize the U.S.A.," *The Reader's Digest*, January, 1963, pp. 79, 81.

and the fact that it interrupts the continuity of programs in which we are interested. It does exercise a censorial force that can be plain niggling, though it could be debated whether this force vitiates or improves the programming. And it *is* paying for the programs. Generally, the talent expended on advertising, and the money, produce commercials which are witty, dull, engrossing, tasteless, exciting, or blah, with a great deal of often delightful music, some innocuous lyrics, and no evident qualities which would seriously debase society.

But there are defects in advertising, cumulative ones, which could shape ideals and attitudes not in conformity with Christian truth, and which could harm both parents and children, particularly if the home and school are not doing their job. The most noteworthy defect of advertising, as I see it, is that it makes us think there is no more drudgery left in life. From washing diapers to bearing children, everything in life is easy. A Kay bass and cello ad announces, "Twice as Easy to Play." Daily we see dirt and bugs, offensive odors, and squadrons of tooth cavities swept away in a trice by the shamanism of advertising. Cooking, cleaning, painting, ironing, making friends, being devilishly popular, wowing the ladies and gents, being in brief consummately happy—it's all a breeze. At least we'd like to think it is. That's why we stock our bookshelves with those how-to-do-it-easy books, the ones with such titles as *30 Days to a More Powerful Vocabulary, Three Weeks to a Better Memory, How to Get Rich in Spite of Yourself, Make a Million While Lying in Bed,* and so on. The only lying involved in making a million dollars is being done by the writer who tells us that it's easy. But little of true value in life is easy, least of all persevering in one's duty for years on end. Persevering—the thought that terrified Ignatius of Loyola, and how many other saints! Persevering—the hallmark of character and the least easy thing in life! It would be too

much to expect that advertising could take the need for per-
severance into account when framing commercials. Perhaps
it shouldn't even try. If the homes and schools and churches
do not teach this value to the young, I doubt that they shall
ever learn it, no matter how much or little advertising they
encounter.

Television commercials may give children queer notions
of what family relationships, and human relationships in
general, should be. When the kids see that margarine brat
sass his father after being warned a second time not to wear
his crown to table, what lesson will they draw? Personally,
I would have bashed that smug little fellow right on his
Imperial crown. And why must there be so much squawking
and yelling in the advertisers' scenes of family life? Does it
tell us something about the homelife of the copywriters?
Life as I have experienced it is not lived at the top of one's
lungs the way the ads depict it—and many of the programs
too, for that matter. It occurs to me that what we have here
is a typical American trait: If you want to get attention,
just raise your voice. May I suggest that we have now
reached that topmost level of sound waves beyond which
no one can hear us, save only dogs and an occasional bat.
Let us all lower our voices, starting with commercials.

I note that advertising is making a genuine effort to be
fair, to be unsegregated. Minority group members are reg-
ularly appearing at commercial cocktail parties and puffing
cigarettes right in the mainstream. It's all to the good,
though they should recognize that they will necessarily
share in the hangovers and emphysema that ensue from
such mainstream activities. The reaction of the minorities
to this development has been expectedly mixed. One result
is the formation of the Mexican-American Anti-Defamation
Committee. Its non-salaried chairman, Nick Reyes of the
Equal Employment Opportunity Commission, has complained of the "image" the commercials project of the Mex-

ican-American. He singled out for criticism our beloved Jose Jimenez, who has of late been urging us to consult the "jellow pages." I wonder what Reyes thinks of that dog food commercial in which a Mexican customs officer, in full-dress uniform, pirates a gringo's dog viands and feeds them to his own mutt? And what about that lovely senorita who scolds her husband for his laziness while he sits idly astride a swaybacked old nag and puffs contentedly on an "L and Eeem"?

"Twenty years ago," complained a spokesman for the Mexican-American committee, "you had quite a lot of advertising using Negroes in a demeaning fashion. Then came the Indians and they protested. Now, it seems the Mexican-American is the new person used for advertising." Indications are that the Frito Bandido is headed for extinction, along with Little Black Sambo and Aunt Jemimah. And the drunken Irishman and miserly Scot. And the stuffy, priggish Englishman and amorous Frenchman. And the conniving Turk and the haggling Jew. The only caricature that seems safe at the moment is that of the "typical German," with his heavy accent and dictatorial ways. Now I ask you, is that fair? My grandfather Trierweiler wouldn't think so, if he were here today. And that portion of my own blood which is Teutonic is beginning to stir uneasily. As long as we're stewing down our culture into a canned soup in which everything tastes the same, why not blend in the German sauerkraut? Perhaps a letter to Rowan and Martin would be just the thing. Veddy interesting.

We Americans have been justly criticized for making too much of eccentricity, oddness, the unusual. We tend to gawk at harelips and ogle hunchbacks, though the reason may be that we see so few of them as compared to other countries. Still we stare at them. Now here come the commercials, urging us not only to notice the unusual and the offbeat, but actually inviting us to make frank comments about it. "Honey, I can't stand your breath." "You have body odor, boss." "Miss Ames, your teeth are dull." "Dearest, you smell like a moose." And so on, into the dark night of the soul. Manners, not morals, often seem in ads to be the bedrock of society. As a result, many of us go about forever wondering what other people think of us. Foreign policy has been conducted on that basis for years.

Even hallowed university halls are tainted by this tendency to conformity. "I know for a fact," Seymour Gross has written, "that one young instructor at a State university was told by the head of his department to take sunlamp treatments [don't be a paleface]; another was told to cut off the beard he had grown over the summer vacation; and another was not hired (I heard this with my own ears!) because he was 'bald as a billiard ball.' " [2]

Before we exile the hippies and flower children, perhaps we should find out exactly what it is about our society that they object to. Who knows, they may just have a point. The kindly and generous way they treat one another, a phenomenon often noted by observers, is in startling contrast to the bad manners displayed by these fastidious denizens of the TV ads who are so easily offended by halitosis and sweat and dirt and who do not hesitate to say so. I should think it better, when assessing our neighbor, to ask a question like, "Is he good?" rather than, "Does he stink?" Years ago Christopher Dawson warned us that television breeds conformism. We are forewarned.

The *Wall Street Journal* some time back presented the short and sad biography of an excellent new dairy product that was marketed by an Eastern firm with great hope and fanfare. The new product, low on calories and fat, was designed for people who are growing old. It appeared about the time that "cholesterol" first threatened to become a

[2] Seymour L. Gross, "Amid the Alien Corn," *America*, Jan. 17, 1959, pp. 457, 458.

family byword. Advertising messages that accompanied the product informed the reader or listener that the product was, quite frankly, meant for the aging, the elderly, those who are over the hill, who must watch their cholesterol intake lest they be stricken suddenly by some wicked infarction. The product flopped. Few bought it, feeling that to do so was an admission of a very unhappy truth: "I am growing old." We don't like to think about that. Hence, advertising usually avoids unpleasantries. "Sugar is energy," the candy ad declares. It doesn't mention the factor of diabetes or tooth decay. Young men are shown quaffing milk by the quart, yet my doctor (a urologist) informs me that, after the age of 18 or 19, the human body simply can't absorb all that milk, nor does it need the calcium. Most of it is excess waste, a burden to the kidneys. But the dairy ads don't mention that. Nor do cigarette ads bring up lung cancer and emphysema. Coffee commercials naturally ignore the fact that some medical men believe the effects of coffee as a beverage are altogether bad. And if the prolonged use of liquid dietary drinks as a substitute for food should perchance induce a severe condition of constipation, we should not expect the commercials to advise us of that possibility.

Advertisers are not the only ones guilty of oversimplification. Freud's pansexualism is a form of it. Thorstein Veblen was an ardent simplifier when he attempted to explain the development of human life and the social structure in terms of living tissue and material environment. These men, and others like them, are more guilty than ad men. The latter cannot afford to devote sufficient time in their commercials to explain all its facets, even if they wanted to. But the consumer can be on his toes when he hears, "Borrow confidently from H.F.C." He can be confident of what will happen if he doesn't repay the loan on the appointed hour.

Another fault of advertising is that it emphasizes action at the expense of contemplation, particularly that portion of it aimed at the adolescent audience. The ad writers apparently feel that young people have little taste for meditating on the verities. I think they are underestimating the young. True adventure, it has been pointed out, lies in the mind of man as he ranges over the landscape of knowledge, making his own the very best that has been thought and said and then building something of his own at the top. I think young people today realize that truth much sooner than we did twenty or thirty years ago. Back in 1957, the Rev. Frederick B. Kellogg, Episcopal chaplain at Harvard, remarked, "Young people are thinking of and wanting more *in*formation rather than formation. People can no longer wait until they're 30 or 35 to know what the purpose of life is. The problem has moved down to the freshman and sophomore." [3] And that was twelve years ago. After teaching for five years in a high school for boys, I would say that the problem, as Rev. Kellogg terms it, has penetrated there as well. Advertisers, for their own good, must take into account the intellectual maturity of the adolescent, lest they be guilty of aping the monosyllabic primers of the progressive schools. Instead of turning the youngster into an enthusiast for learning, they simply turned him off. I don't think ad men want to do that.

In 1960 the anthropophagous Malcolm Muggeridge, perennial demolition expert of our "motel" culture, selected what he thought was the best cartoon to appear in the magazine *Punch* in the preceding five years. His choice showed a man hunched in a chair, one hand to his chin, the other hand caressing a cigarette. He was staring vacantly at a television screen. The cartoon was titled, *Le Non-Penseur*. Sir Malcolm is deeply prejudiced against this stereotype of modern man. I wonder why? Perhaps we have here additional proof of the theory of Gerhart Saenger and Samuel Flowerman, who contend that we are not preju-

[3] Quoted in *Newsweek*, April 22, 1957, p. 120.

diced against the "typical Jew" or the "typical Italian" (or the "typical non-thinker"?) because he is different from us. On the contrary. The very qualities which we object to in him are the same attributes we find, and prize, in ourselves. Could it be that we despise him because he so honestly and painfully mirrors ourselves? I must ask Sir Malcolm about that one day.

Meanwhile I reject his stereotype, as one must reject all stereotypes, for they are not accurate representations of men. They are merely easy targets on which disgruntled and bilious critics can vent their literary flatulence. Modern man may not be a "magazine of the arts," but he has emerged well clean of much of the superstition, ignorance, and bigotry that have marked his past, even in England. And advertising, with all its faults, has played a part in that emergence.

There is no reason to despair or fret over Sir Malcolm's cartoon man idling before the television screen. Is his stare vacant? Is he reacting to what goes on before him? Then let us apply a device by which we can measure his capillary response. Or give him a galvanic skin-response test. Or take his pulse. And even if the results of all our tests prove to be negative and we find that the stare enameling his features is indeed vacant, what does that prove? Perhaps he is adventuring at all those resorts and spas of thought that the TV itinerary so often overlooks as it makes its daily tour. If his face were alive and rapt before the TV screen, then, I think, we might have real reason to worry.

CHAPTER 11

His Excellency, the Pipsqueak

The host at Cana's marriage feast was criticized for saving the best till last. I have followed his example—almost; not as the result of a miracle, however, but simply because the subject of this chapter is exalted, essential, unique, unexpendable. I mean the priesthood. And we will take a gander at some vocations advertisements too, and find out if any of that Madison Avenue smog has settled out on them.

To begin with, let us accept the fact that there is a shortage of vocations. No doubt of it. But why? Answering that will take some doing. It is often said that vocations are made in heaven. Rubbish! Vocations are made on earth. They are made on earth by kind and virtuous priests and religious who in their shining example give youth eloquent tangible evidence, a visual glimpse if you will, of the beauty of a life consecrated to the service of God. Vocations are made in heaven? No they aren't. They are made on earth by self-sacrificing, virtuous parents whose everyday lives are saturated with the very heroism needed by priests and religious. Vocations are made in heaven? Not at all. They are made right here on earth. They are certified in heaven. God seals the vocation, stamps it as genuine, through the ordaining bishop or through the religious superior who accepts a profession of vows. If vocations were made in heaven, why we could comfortably blame the present shortage of them on What's-His-name.

Not everyone agrees with that, as you might expect. Herewith an example:

> Vocation ads, it has been recognized, are one of the major deterrents to the religious state. Nor has such advertising noticeably improved in the post-council period . . . It is to say nothing new to point out the emphasis on adolescent values such ads reveal; though in this there may be a key to the frustrations mature religious experience in the apparently prevalent teen-age atmosphere of some communities. What is undoubtedly more noteworthy is the fact that the quantity of vocation advertising in a given magazine is in inverse ratio to its intellectual quality; so that, to take an immediate example, *The Messenger of the Sacred Heart* would carry three times more ads than, say, *Sign,* which in turn would carry three times more than *Commonweal,* etc. What this says about the calibre of candidate the religious institutes themselves are seeking to attract requires no elaboration.[1]

Whew! Even the little tailor of fairy tale fame didn't clobber many more with a single blow than the writer of this paragraph. He has managed to indict vocation advertisements as a "major" reason for the shortage of aspirants to the religious life, many religious communities for being adolescent in spirit, *The Messenger of the Sacred Heart* (R.I.P.) for its low intellectual quality, candidates for the religious life for being, one assumes, either shallow or puerile or both, and the communities themselves for actually beating the bushes in search of such mental duds. It fairly takes one's breath away.

The alarming dearth of young people who want to be priests, nuns, or brothers is, as I have said, a fact of life. To put the picture into focus, however, we should note that a number of students of this phenomenon point out that the

[1] "The Cellophane Epiphany," *Jubilee,* Jan., 1968, p. 27.

desideratum in regard to religious is quality, not quantity. Whether or not quality and quantity can coexist at one and the same time is as much a perplexity in the seminary world as it is in the field of education in general. At least we shouldn't be flabbergasted if hordes of young people are not breaking down convent doors in order to "come, follow me." And I might point out that an astonishing and fascinating study could be made of the young men and women who have answered Christ's call and, in spite of themselves, been turned away by seminary authorities for one reason or another. The meat of this hypothetical study would be the reasons why the authorities rejected or expelled the candidates, reasons, by the way, which most seminaries "reserve the right" to keep secret, even from the expellee himself! I am not saying that their reasons for dropping aspirants were bad, but only that they bear analysis. In one midwestern seminary, 36 young men began studies for the priesthood in the first-year college division. At the beginning of each succeeding year, new faces appeared as men who had done one or more years of college elsewhere, or who already had their degrees, entered the seminary to begin training. At the end of eight years, from this class which numbered, all told, well above 100 seminarians, the archbishop ordained *one man.*

Ascribing the lack of vocations to vocational advertising indicates to me a certain unawareness of problems relevant to seminary life and to the life of the Church. To illustrate. A few years ago a group of Jesuit theologians developed a program called "Jesuit Contacts." They wrote to many dioceses within the provinces of their order, asking permission to send one poster per month to the high schools and colleges in these dioceses. The posters would tell some facts about Jesuit life. An innocent enough request, one would think, and surely in keeping with the apostolic spirit of Christ. Yet three dioceses (Denver, St. Paul, and Dubuque) turned the request down flat, and almost half the dioceses in the Wisconsin province didn't bother to answer the query.

Jealousy in the vineyard? It wouldn't be the first time. The bitter animosity of the Denver Archdiocese toward the Jesuits in past years, a policy which originated in the most inner sanctum of the chancery office, is all the more inexplicable when we reflect that the majority of vocations to the secular priesthood in that diocese emanate from Jesuit schools. In the fall of 1955, for example, the archbishop (since retired) complained to his director of vocations, Father Bert Woodrich, saying he was "very unhappy" that all the Denver vocations were from Regis High (run by the Jesuits), and that none of the other archdiocesan high schools was represented. Jealousy in the vineyard? How could it be? When Father Woodrich was appointed director of vocations, the first man to send him a congratulatory message, which promised "full cooperation" of the faculty at Regis, was the president of Regis College, Father Richard Ryan, a Jesuit.

When *Jubilee* magazine calls vocational advertising a "major deterrent to the religious state," it is "fishing for trout in a hot spring." It had better look elsewhere: at a diocesan seminary on whose grounds members of some other religious orders were forbidden to set foot. Or perhaps at an archdiocesan seminary where theologians were publicly forbidden to choose as their spiritual director any priest who was not a member of the seminary faculty. This rule, which came from the rector of that seminary, is not technically in conflict with Canon Law (c. 1361, §1), which stipulates that the seminary officials will designate those confessors to whom the students can "freely" go. It would appear, however, to conflict with a higher law, the law of love. In imposing the rule, the seminary used legalism as a crowbar to lever out religion. For a considerable number of the seminarians affected had been under direction outside the seminary before entering. Many, without that direction, would not have chosen the priesthood at all, and certainly not at this particular seminary. Yet an arbitrary rule forbade them the guidance of their regular confessor and director, under pain of expulsion. One is tempted to ask the officials of such a seminary: Whose side are you on?

Delving deeply into the causes of the lack of vocations is beyond the scope of this book and the capabilities of its author. But I can at least make a suggestion. Solving the shortage of priests, nuns, and brothers will require a long, hard look at the use (or abuse) of ecclesiastical power, both in and out of seminaries. Inside the seminary, fear is very often the overriding emotion, coloring all of a student's life: fear of being expelled, fear of being delated to the authorities, fear of being cut from orders, fear of many punishments, and all of this, mind you, with no explanations given, and often without any prior warning or cautionary suggestion that one should mend one's ways. As one seminary manual puts it, "The seminary reserves the right to dismiss any student at any time, even without stating the cause for the dismissal." [2]

I cannot help but think of a book that appeared nearly 15 years ago, a most perceptive book, years ahead of its time. It was called *Nothing Is Quite Enough*, and its author, Gary MacEoin, had himself been dismissed from a seminary just short of ordination to the priesthood, with no explanations! (This is not unusual. A friend of mine was once dismissed, and when he asked the rector for a reason, that official replied, "Let's call it the X factor.") In a review of MacEoin's book Father Gerald Vann commented:

> . . . a religious Order may or may not be right in rejecting a subject, even without warning and at a very late hour, but at least when it does so it should treat him as a human being, a

[2] Rules, Customs, and Formulary of Prayers of St. Thomas' Seminary (Denver, Colo.), 1951, paragraph 22, "Dismissal."

rational animal: it should give him some rational grounds for its decision. God deals with all things according to their natures: it is tragic when men, in the name of religion, seem to try to go one better than God.[3]

Even in the family circle that is the seminary, a tyrannous father can destroy the spirit of his children, so that the last thing they would think of doing, the very last, would be to go to him with a problem of any sort. "The peculiar characteristic of slavery," said St. Ambrose long ago, "is to be always in fear." We can't say we haven't been warned, can we?

Equally self-deluding are those approaches to the vocation shortage which fix the major portion of the blame on parents. Such a program was launched in the New York Archdiocese in 1960. This so-called "saturation" approach involved a ten-month distribution of vocational literature "addressed not to young folks but to parents." [4] In other words, the key to the shortage of priests is the ignorance of the adult laity! Father Donald F. Miller, one of the ubiquitous *Liguorian* Millers, in an issue of that magazine has raised the question of vocations. He remarks: "It is true that in times of great stress, personality conflict, and economic trouble, the parents of large families are always inclined to speak with almost scornful envy of the freedom from such troubles that marks the lives of religious." [5] With all the gentleness I can muster, I must observe that Father Miller's statement contains two monumental stupidities. The first is his belief that parents of large families always carp at religious in times of *sturm und drang*. How can he possibly know that? How many parents of large families? I have known such parents, a considerable number of them, and I do not remember once hearing them speak disparag-

[3] *Blackfriars*, February, 1955.
[4] "'Saturation' Program for Vocations," *Priest* magazine, Feb., 1960, p. 165.
[5] "Are Young People Being Cheated?" *Liguorian*, Sept., 1966, p. 7.

ingly of the freedom religious enjoy from similar problems. And that brings up the second colossal boner: Since when do religious enjoy freedom from great stress and personality conflict? The words are wild. Religious, if I am not mistaken, are human beings. It is one of the burdens of being human to suffer stress, great and small, and personality conflicts. The only way to escape stress is to die; the only way to escape personality conflicts is to retire to some mountain or desert fastness and there contemplate, far from the madding crowd. Religious who read Father Miller's remarks about their freedom from stress and personality conflicts will be forgiven if they snicker, chortle, or faint. What about religious and economic trouble? The majority, I imagine, do not have any such problem of money. But what of the superiors of schools, whose budgets continue to spiral upward as more and more laity (who demand larger and larger salaries) are added to the payroll? And what of convents, like that of the Poor Clares south of San Francisco, which often go hungry for simple lack of food. I think one could call that an "economic trouble." Until vocations programs, then, turn inward and, in particular, seek to educate, not the parents, but rather the diocesan officials, seminary authorities and faculty, and pastors about the humane and Christian use of power, they will bear no fruit.

Let us look at the vocations advertisements which *Jubilee* magazine found so objectionable, so adolescent. What are these "adolescent" values which they emphasize. An entire page of such advertising is reproduced in the article; it involves recruiting messages from six different communities. The first ad comes from the Priests of the Sacred Heart in Great Barrington, Massachusetts. It reads: "A call may be a command. It depends on the love, the readiness, the courage, the capacity of the hearer to respond." End of commercial. Do you see anything adolescent about love, willingness, courage, and readiness? I don't. These are virtues of a mature individual. Next, the Trappists of Genesee Abbey in New York ask the question, "Where does your treasure lie?" And they reply, "In a life that is integral, prayerful, productive (in work and study), fraternal. As a Trappist monk?" In what sense, pray tell, are integrity, productivity, prayerfulness, and fraternity adolescent values? What would the *Jubilee* writer substitute in their place as mature values: partiality, diffuseness of mind and heart, inertia, and alienation?

The third vocation ad issues from the Holy Family Seminary in St. Louis, Missouri, and it states simply: "There is still time to serve Christ." That's all. Service, we should note, is perhaps one of the most Christlike of virtues. One of the Pope's proudest titles is Servant of the Servants of God. To serve one's fellowman and to serve him well requires humility, deep love, and an inexhaustible capacity for accepting rebuff in good spirits. (Perhaps that helps explain the present shortage of waiters, as well as of priests.)

The advertisement of the Immaculate Heart Missioners begins by saying, "Your future may shape the future of others." And then it lists some of the works performed by its missionaries: feeding the hungry, housing the homeless, educating the young, befriending the friendless, and teaching them Christ. Would a man or youth who answered such a call be of inferior caliber? Would he be adolescent in spirit? And is this congregation adolescent because it seeks men who wish to perform such services? The illustration which accompanies this ad shows various priests carrying out duties for the order: one is driving a jeep, one rowing a native dugout, another riding horseback, and a fourth walking out on the tarmac toward a single engine plane. Missionaries, like most other men, will use whatever form of transportation is feasible and best in the circumstances. Calling attention to that fact in a vocations ad can hardly be called an emphasis of adolescent values.

The vocational ad of the St. Joseph Novitiate at Bailey's Harbor, Wisconsin, is reminiscent of World War II military recruitment posters. It shows a cleric pointing a forefinger directly at the reader, while beneath are the words, "The Sacred Heart Wants You." A middle-aged man will chuckle at this reminder of the "Uncle Sam Wants You" signs that decorated Army and Navy recruiting centers 25 years ago. A rather martial air, true. But does that make it adolescent? It is no less martial than the flavor of the Exercises of St. Ignatius of Loyola, and no one, to my knowledge, has accused the Exercises of being adolescent. Too rigid, perhaps. Too methodical, maybe. Too introspective, could be. Adolescent, never. The last ad is from the Missionaries of the Sacred Heart, Geneva, Illinois. It is illustrated by a drawing of a young priest in a baseball cap, riding a bicycle with a Red-Cross kit on the handlebars. The message is simply, "We are there because we care." Maybe *Jubilee* has a thing about baseball caps on clerics.

What we have just surveyed is a representative sampling of vocational advertising as formulated by American religious communities. What does it reveal? A certain simplicity, I should say. Certainly a desire to win the hearts of men who want to improve their own and others' relationships with Christ. They are not adolescent. Naive, perhaps, in some respects, and certainly amateurish when compared with the high-horsepower recruitment literature printed up by affluent corporations and by the Federal government. But amateurishness, as we shall see, can be a very great blessing. Other vocational ads are of similar quality.

The main criticism to which some vocational advertising leaves itself open is that it tends to confuse the essential function of the priesthood. What the priesthood is all about, what makes it absolutely essential to the Church and to the well-being of the world, has nothing to do with ghettos or suburbs, housing, journalism, education, farm-labor problems, or even mending comminuted fractures. Anyone can tend to those fields and many are. What distinguishes the priesthood, and what makes it so special that mankind can't get along without it, is its role of particularizing and localizing the priestly power of Christ, that power by which we are fed with a more than earthly Bread and strengthened by a more than human grace. That is the difference between the priesthood and a religious order. The order, though it may do great work, is not essential to the Church. The priesthood is. But when a vocations poster reads like an advertisement for the Peace Corps or VISTA, then someone has forgotten for the moment what Cardinal Suhard once observed: "The priesthood is not something, it is *someone:* Christ." We can no more survive without the priesthood than we can survive without Christ. And that, it seems to me, is what vocational advertising for the priesthood should be all about.

But the Claretian Fathers in Chicago seem not to agree. Their founder, St. Anthony Claret, had given some 10,000 sermons and written perhaps 200 books and pamphlets by the time of his death in 1870. He is in every way a "patron of the Catholic press." But what have his sons done to his blessed memory? They have come up with a vocations ad that attempts to build the stature of the congregation by slyly knocking the reputations of other, more familiar orders. It begins by announcing in bold Bodoni letters: "We never burned anybody at the stake." And then it presents the following paid message:

When one of our enthusiastic young priests starts rubbing ideas together, we don't tie him down down. Our congregation, founded in 1849, is too young to be bound by traditions from the Middle Ages and the Renaissance. With 6,000 members throughout the world—priests, students and brothers—we're big enough to be effective, small enough to be flexible. We like to go where the heat's on: in the inner city, in underdeveloped countries overseas, on secular university campuses, in journalism and publishing. If you warm to our kind of work, join us. Talk it over with our vocations director, Father Lawrence Hoge.

I think I would encourage any promising young man to join the Claretians, but it would be in spite of, not because of, this flashy, slick, hip, smelling-of-the-big-time-ad-agency stew of flimflam and veiled insult. What on earth possessed Father Hoge? (Call him collect at 312-236-7782.) There seems to be only one explanation: he summoned the Jack Tinker Agency or BBB&D, or some other Madison Avenue powerhouse of logorrhea, and said, "Now look here, fellas. Give me a vocations pitch that really swings. I mean, put it in the 20th century, dig? The young cats don't buy us, baby, so dream us up a groovy thing that really moves." And they did.

To compound the felony, the Claretian advertisement features as its only art work a photograph of a book of matches, opened, with one lonely half-burned match lying loose—perhaps the very match that touched off the faggots under some poor heretic. (I'll bet it wasn't a Claretian who did it.) I hope that when the ad agency sent its bill to the Claretians for this production, it gave them a clergy discount.

A group of archaelogists some years ago quickly discovered, from a study of aerial photographs, the ancient ruins of a jungle city that they had been unable to detect from the ground, even though they had walked directly over them. In this age of microspecialization, perhaps like the archaeologists we need to get farther away from our subject, the "vocation crisis," in order to see it clearly, in its causes. We need a better vantage point both philosophically and historically, to arrive at proper diagnosis and treatment. That is a task for wiser heads than mine.

But there is a coign of vantage from which we can get a

better look at the subject. I mean that hoary old meta-physical concept of the chain of being in the universe, that web of relationships that connects all reality and establishes it in an interacting hierarchy. What it means is that disparate things are somehow related, if we look hard enough. For instance one phenomenon (say, a student riot at the Sorbonne in Paris) may well be related in its causes to another phenomenon (say, the secreting of a tape recorder by seminarians at a faculty meeting in order to obtain top-secret information about who will be called to orders, who will not, and why). The common denominator might be, as they say at the top, an erosion of the virtue of obedience on the part of the governed. Or it might be that authority has not earned obedience, a concept that has received precious little publicity in the swelling corpus of literature on the virtues. Modern youth are not interested in planting and watering walking sticks in a monastery garden just because an abbot commands it. There must be some value to the thing commanded, some rationale supporting it, even though the one commanding merits obedience by virtue of divine law or a vow. It has been said that subjects can go to hell for disobeying. And rulers can as readily go to hell for commanding. We should be concerned today with the *quality* of obedience and the quality of authority (particularly the latter) if we want to understand the shortage of vocations.

It's not that there are fewer young men. Dr. Conrad Taeuber, assistant director of the Census Bureau, recently released figures which show that the fastest growing segment of the population is that between ages 20 and 34. He estimates that by 1978 the median age in the United States will be 27. What a tragic irony. In the very era when the numbers of youth are multiplying beyond a discotheque owner's wildest hopes, fewer and fewer of them show an interest in the priesthood and the religious life.

I suspect we're not getting the picture across to them. It

is not a failure of advertising or of literature but of living. And it is closely related to other tendencies in society. When numbers of intellectual Catholics today attempt to redefine the Church as little more than an arm of the Department of Health, Education, and Welfare, the idea of priesthood, to no one's amazement, will begin to bear a marked resemblance to that of social worker. And we may even say that a vocations advertisement will read like a civil service job description. Is that the image bishops and priests project today to youth?

Defining the Church in secular terms has become almost a passion among some Catholic, not to mention Protestant, writers. They describe "confrontation" with the world and one's neighbor in rapturous periods heretofore limited to our sacramental union with Christ in the Eucharist. Some seem to resent the idea that Christ is more richly present in the Mass than in our fellow man. Poetic imagery, always a threat to the logical development of ideas, is usurping in their works the role of formal theological terms. As when they speak of "the sacrament of our neighbor," or the "liturgy of love." "Even beer is sacred," I read recently on a Catholic editorial page.

The trouble with symbolic language is that it is symbolic. That is, it is only partly true. But which part? It is ambiguous, misleading, and imprecise. Poets have never bothered much about making "fine" distinctions (like the difference between Nature and God), even in that bygone era when they tried to communicate ideas and experiences. Nowadays, I am told, they have sequestered themselves deep in the caverns of unintelligibility. There they are analyzing shadows cast by the fire on the walls of the cave in an effort to explain the enigma of reality. If a part of the essence of poetry is unspecifiability, or indeterminancy, and I think it is, then it makes a rather shaky vehicle in which to transport something as fragile as accurate knowledge of God and His Church.

The anomaly is that writers who want to secularize the Church are often hailed as forward looking, as having their eyes fixed on Omega. In reality they are looking backward to Alpha, or more precisely to Mu. What they are trying to achieve is a revival of the Medieval situation, that is, the participation of the Church in the work of the laity, the secular world of politics, legislative action, diplomacy, urban development, etc. Catholic action, by which I mean the participation of the laity in the work of the Church, was relatively rare in the Middle Ages. Quite the reverse. It was the Church that participated (or interfered, depending on your point of view) in the work of the layman. Then there were bishops and priests in politics, perhaps because no layman was available who could handle the job. (Not the case today, however.) Bishops led troops into battle, wearing full armor and swinging maces and broadswords with a vigor altogether secular. Ecclesiastics were commonly diplomats and statesmen. In general, civil responsibility was assumed often and everywhere by the Church and the clergy, no clear distinction being made between the temporal and eternal kingdoms. They were but two aspects of a single Christian State.

The secularists would appear to desire a revival of that state of affairs—but with certain provisos. I have noted that when a bishop or other ecclesiastic obtrudes in the world of purely secular and mundane affairs, he is praised or blamed by the secularists in accordance with whether his recommendations agree or disagree with theirs. We may say that the participation in the world which the secularists demand of clerics is only a partial and conditional one, predicated on the assumption that the clergy will faithfully follow the secularists' prescriptions. If they do, then they are cordially invited to jump with both feet into the temporal melee.

I can't imagine that vocations will be nurtured and increased by telling young men about their priestly function, for example, in politics. They may view politics, in the words of a former mayor of Manila, as "a way of looking at life through a garbage can." A student, journalist, athlete, policeman, or welfare worker will not be wooed to a true vision of the glories of the priesthood by a vocations ad that assures him he will be sent to "the inner city where the heat's on." What he wants is not heat in the inner (or outer) city, but a sharing in the eternal priesthood, *wherever it may take him.* What he wants is light, the light of a clear picture of just what it means to be a priest of Jesus Christ, the only irreplaceable man.

No writer in a Christian and Catholic context today can mention authority, as I did a few pages ago, without calling up visions of sandbagged bishops, peeping warily over chancery parapets to see who's going to fire off the next barrage of billingsgate. Like most other wielders of authority, bishops are under heavy fire. They are getting a bad press. Some of it, of course, they deserve. Some of it they don't. Cardinal McIntyre of Los Angeles comes to mind. A priest of the San Diego diocese, who has spent years in welfare work of all sorts, remarked to me, "I wish that writers who pillory Cardinal McIntyre could know from personal experience, as I do, of the thousands and thousands of people he has helped in his years in Los Angeles." And he described to me instances of personal assistance, not simply the flourishing of the metropolitan fountain pen over the archdiocesan checkbook. Such charity rarely comes to light. I am afraid that today a man cannot find favor in the press by helping *people.* He must help *causes.* When a bishop resurrects dead faith, dead hope, dead ideals, and dead marriages, the men on the copy desks of city newspapers simply yawn and wonder when the next riot will erupt. But let a bishop fail to espouse a cause, even a cause whose merit is disputed by good and able men, and the reporters begin to sharpen their pencils and their innuendo.

Some Catholic reporters are perhaps less kind, particularly if their sources are individuals who feel that a bishop has treated them unjustly or maliciously. The picture of the typical bishop that takes shape in the pages of these papers is more of a caricature than a portrait. And caricatures are the work of cartoonists, whose metier is exaggeration. The impression is being conveyed that to be a bishop is to be a tyrant. It's not a new misconception, of course. Once, in speaking of a politician who was arrogant and domineering, Abraham Lincoln commented, "Sumner is my idea of a bishop." And we may go back much farther than Lincoln. Origen, that genius of the early Church and a man of encyclopedic learning, once wrote of some bishops of his day:

> There are times when we outdo in pride the evil princes of the heathens. A little more of this and we, like the king, will have to have a bodyguard. Terror dogs our steps. We live apart, inaccessible to everyone—and in particular to the poor. To those who seek our help we are haughtier than any despot, than even the cruelest of kings. Such is the condition of affairs in many a famous Church, particularly in the Churches of our most noted cities.

So there were tares in the Church, even so long ago, when the dust stirred up by the feet of men who had laid their eyes on Christ had only just begun to settle. Tares among the successors to the Apostles! And there was Judas, handpicked by Himself. So we won't expect absolute perfection, not just yet, not anywhere in the world or in the Church.

What is your idea of a bishop? What forces have shaped it? Ordinarily we form our ideas of a class of men by the results of personal contacts with individual members of that class. Our contacts with bishops, I regret to say, are well below the "x" axis on standard coordinate paper. Or to put it another way, His Excellency went thattaway. The average bishop's remoteness from his people is an inevitable corollary of his equating episcopacy with administration. He is not the shepherd but the owner of the sheep ranch, up in his office overseeing plans for a new corral and counting the tally from the last sale of wool. And his example is contagious; he sets the mood of the diocese. I know intimately an elderly couple in Denver who have lived for 28 years in the same house, in the same parish, under the same pastor. They have raised two sons in the faith, sent them to Catholic high schools and colleges, and supported all parish and diocesan "projects" at great personal sacrifice. Yet in those 28 years, their pastor has never entered their home, nor have any of his assistants. Their pastor, I fear, has become merely the man to whom they gave their money and who has used (or abused) it. He is in no way a shepherd to them. *A fortiori* the bishop. To many Catholics, a bishop is just an astronautical priest who has been put into orbit by Rome in the outer space of high finance and executive finagling. They wouldn't know how to talk to him, even if they should get the chance. He would be as alien in their living room as some teratoid creature lately landed from Venus or Mars.

Since the people's contacts with their bishop are miniscule, what other forces are there which shape their image of him? Mostly books, magazines, articles, hearsay, and the popular press, religious and secular. To which list we may add television news and commentary. The purpose of the media of communication is not to create a favorable image of Catholic bishops, or any other kind. Not even the religious press should engage in such an adventurous enterprise. There was a time when it did, exhaustively, relentlessly, with considerable editing or suppression of the facts.

Somewhere there must exist a happy medium between whitewash and sensational exposé. Each journalistic "image maker" bears the onerous responsibility of arriving at that delicate mean. I wish him success. I wish that when the time comes for him to make an accounting of his stewardship of the typewriter, he may utter as his own the words of Paul Claudel:

> It will be sweet to me on my deathbed to think that my books have not added to the terrible sum of darkness, doubt, and impurity that afflicts humanity, but that those who read them could not but find in them reasons to believe, to hope, and to rejoice.

Conservative Catholics may ask if the editors of the *National Catholic Reporter* will have much to rejoice about when they are on their deathbeds. Because of its readiness to make "sacristy gossip" a part of the public domain, *NCR* has infuriated ecclesiastics and laymen by the boatload. It has been called a spokesman for the devil, a shipworm in the Bark of Peter, a picador of Roman bulls, a baiter of bishops, and a boll weevil with a tapeworm set loose in the Golden Fleece. Whether such placid criticism is warranted or not, there are some things that we should thank *NCR* for doing.

To begin with, its emergence was a predictable reaction to the despotic state of affairs that obtained in the Catholic press in days gone by. Our imagination boggles to think of a time when no criticism was allowed in diocesan newspapers of such matters as Legion of Decency judgments of films or episcopal policy in regard to building. But such criticism was often sorely needed. In a Rocky Mountain archdiocese, the bishop permitted only one architect to design schools and churches. I know of only one pastor who evaded this puzzling "law," and he did so by submitting two unnamed bids. The bishop chose the lower bid, and by the time he discovered that it was not the work of his special architect, work was already under way; it was too late for him to reverse his decision. In another diocese in the Southwest, most of the construction work on all Church projects was contracted out to a company owned by the bishop's brother. No criticism of such nearsighted policies, as you might expect, was forthcoming in the diocesan press. Priests sniggered at or cursed such policies in the privacy of 40 Hours' get-togethers (when the bishop was not around), at church dedications, and retreats. But that was as far as the matter went.

And this tyranny filtered down into the most picayunish areas. A certain Bishop of Cheyenne, Wyoming, once sent his editor a note forbidding any further use of two-column type in his diocesan newspaper. He probably felt that the charisma conferred on him by consecration was equivalent to a couple of semesters at a journalism school. Another Catholic publisher for more than a quarter of a century refused to permit the word "honeymoon" to appear in his papers. "Wedding trip" was always substituted by copy editors. Imagine what such a rule would do to song writers! Editorials, of course, were rigorously censored so that no "dangerous" topics might appear, such as evolution (except to deny it), the difference between a law and a probability, whether the tobacco mosaic virus was living or non-living, etc. There were always plenty of saints (stolen from Alban Butler), answers to dogmatic questions (stolen from Noldin), and answers to moral perplexities (stolen from Joné). Plus the usual diocesan chitchat, pictures of new buildings, and, at least once per issue, a picture of the bishop, just to assure the faithful that he really did exist. *NCR*'s presence, then, was as predictable as the bruise on a prize-fighter's face.

The chief benefit, as I see it, that the Catholic world has gotten from *NCR* is the result of its very penchant for

splashing sacristy gossip all over page one. If there are any
bishops left who are unjust, uncharitable, and cruel in their
dealings with priests and people, they will now think twice
(or even three times) before they come to decisions involv-
ing others. *NCR,* whether we like it or not, has brought
out into the fresh air a truth that was shut up in the closet
too long; namely, that a bishop by his decisions is affecting,
or afflicting, persons, individual souls, each as important to
God as the bishop himself. He can no longer command *anything* and expect obedience. One bishop in the Far West
refused to give his imprimatur to a young priest's book until
he changed the title. "The title you have," the bishop wrote,
"doesn't appeal to me." *NCR* has helped us struggle out of
that authoritarian morass in which a bishop governed by
what "appealed" to him. If he is to receive obedience now,
he must "recommend his authority" (the phrase is Archbishop Thomas Roberts'); he must present authority as
worthy of our obedience.

Some readers may construe what I have been saying
as a subtle or perhaps ham-handed attack on the apostolic
succession of the episcopacy, or on the jurisdiction of bishops
as given them by Christ, or some such thing. After all,
Christ commanded Peter to pitch his nets into the water
even though it was Peter who was the master fisherman and
Jesus only a carpenter. Peter knew the fish, the waves,
and the weather; Jesus, only adzes and saws and the grain
of woods. Yet the builder of tables instructed the grizzled
fisherman about the ways of fish, and Peter, reluctantly
it seems, obeyed in spite of misgivings. The result was
an immense haul of fish. Which goes to show that man's
second or third choice is often God's first.

All true enough. But we can get into deep water if we
try to apply a Gospel story lock, stock, and barrel to a
present situation. The stories teach a general truth, in this
case, the rewards attached to obeying Christ. But this

miracle of fishes does not mean that a Christian should obey *whatever* a bishop commands. Nor does it free a bishop of his responsibility to see that his commands are as well-reasoned and intelligent as he can make them. He is, after all, a successor to the apostles. He is not an apostle. He has the fulness of Christ's priesthood. He is not Christ. Christ could look at the waters and say to Peter, "Fish here." The bishop had better consult the *Farmer's Almanac,* the Bureau of Fisheries, and the Coast Guard before he tells us other-Peters where to drop our nets.

I have read that in ancient Rome victorious generals returning to the capital from their campaigns were often met by tumultuous adulation from the multitudes of people. So head-turning was this applause that a man was appointed to ride in the general's chariot as he made his way through the cheering crowds, and to repeat to the general, "Remember, you are only a man." I suppose the Emperor didn't want any upstart military brass crowding into his own divine territory. Now I wonder if Rome, when it appoints a bishop, couldn't also appoint some free soul to stay at the bishop's side and repeat to him, at least once an hour, "Your Excellency, you are a pipsqueak." I think bishops need to be reminded of that. All the rest of us are: by petulant youngsters, cross wives, demanding bosses, thersitical foremen, surly clerks and waitresses, and by the reigning intelligentsia. A bishop unfortunately has no one to tell him he is a pipsqueak. He needs to know. We all do. It is imperative if we are to have any humility. "Your Excellency, you are a pipsqueak." It has a nice ring to it. "Your Eminence, you are a pipsqueak." The words roll trippingly from the tongue. "Your holiness, you are . . ." But I go too far.

Christ invested his spiritual authority in a group of men and in those who have succeeded them, and that is a fact of faith, whether those men were cowards, heroes, lechers, saints, or pipsqueaks. But these men, who are our bishops, must recommend their authority. We automatically respect the office; the man must earn our respect. He can do so by commanding lovingly, intelligently, with the most tender compassion for our problems. If he does that, we will obey freely and with abandon. At least, most of us will.

I say "most of us will" since even the august and divine presence of Christ could not guarantee 100% obedience among His followers in Palestine. Judas' defection, to the best of my knowledge, has not yet been blamed on an abuse of authority by Christ our Lord.

Vocations advertising is a major deterrent to the religious state, says the *Jubilee* writer. I doubt it. At least no priest or religious to whom I have talked has ever cited these ads as a factor in the decline of vocations. They have cited many other things such as the general trend of our culture, a deterioration of family life, abuse of authority, crisis of obedience, the quality of seminary training, and even "the use of psychological testing, psychiatric interview, ability testing, and vocational interest testing, along with more varied interviewing techniques." [6] But vocations ads? Never. One religious superior, when I questioned her about the ads, replied that they might, in some cases, help direct a person already interested in religious life to a particular congregation. She doubted that they had anything to do with that interest itself, and therein lies the crux of the problem.

In a season of almost Dionysiac criticism of the Church, it is hardly surprising that vocations ads should receive their meed of damns, that they should inspire hieratic Hawkshaws to murmur somberly, "Meanwhile, in their pursuit of recruits, the religious orders sing a song of American salesmanship." [7] Such comments almost make one reply, "Would to

[6] *Sister Formation Bulletin,* official publication of the National Sister Formation Conference, Spring, 1968, p. 2.

[7] Edward Wakin and Father Joseph F. Scheuer, *The De-Romanization of the American Catholic Church* (New York: The Macmillan Company, 1966), p. 147.

God that they did!" For "American salesmanship" is a part of that total industrial package which, if you can believe Jean-Jacques Servan-Schreiber, is about to establish an American cultural monopoly in the world. Vocations ads are hardly in that class. They are far from establishing a monopoly on anything, not even column inches in pious magazines, now that the *Sacred Heart Messenger* has bit the dust.

Finally, vocations ads are not, as Wakin and Scheuer would have it, a stepping on the toes of the Holy Ghost by vocations directors who feel that the Spirit has muffed His job, that His territory should be taken over by men more knowledgeable in marketing techniques. To be sure, the Holy Ghost has been given us to "guide us to all truth," even including the truth of whether we should become a priest or religious. But He is just that and no more, a guide, a divine one of course. Yet, even when a man is provided with a guide, he may still need the help of a cane or crutch —and sometimes a shove in the back.

The Myth of American Materialism

An Epilogue

No one was surprised when a Princeton University economist in 1963 quoted Shakespeare in support of an immediate cut in the income tax. ("If it were done when 'tis done, then 'twere well it were done quickly.") The Bard of Avon, like Arthur Schlesinger, Jr., has something to say about everything. The quotation, by the way, is from *Macbeth,* a play which, to judge from the present climate of hysteria, may never be produced again and will surely be excised forever from high school literary texts. For it is full of racial prejudice (those dirty Scots!) and of war. Violence runs rampant in it: against authority (King Duncan), friends (Banquo), children (Ross, son of Macduff), women (Lady Macduff), and even, dare I say it, against animals! Many of them were cruelly vivisected for service in the witches' bubbling cauldron. To top it all, the villain of the piece, Macbeth himself, ends up with his head chopped off. As though capital punishment ever reformed a criminal! What he really needed was a term in a progressive prison where, with therapeutic analysis, he could have learned his real identity, mastered a useful trade, and emerged in a few years ready to dive responsibly into the mainstream, making license plates or printing handbills to support himself. (He would, of course, have divorced his wife and solved *that* problem.)

Macbeth is unblushingly macabre as it narrates the sanguinary story of a man who achieves his wicked ambitions with the aid of a good sharp knife and a sharp-tongued wife. Shakespeare has woven through the plot a counterpoint of magic and sorcery not only to flatter the royal specialist in demonology, King James I, and titillate the taste of a spook-ridden Elizabethan audience, but also to bring into focus the central issue of life: Good and evil, heaven and hell, are at war in every human soul.

What a rousing story it is! Witches croon their malevolent chant and celebrate a cabalistic liturgy. Banquo metastasizes in ghostly form, like a nagging conscience, and throws the royal banquet into an uproar. Lady Macbeth drifts like a shadow through the palace darkness, trying to wash the blood of the past off her hands. And at last the drama dissolves into a phantasmagoria of battle flags, alarums, castle parapets, and clashing armies, the whole clangorous ensemble catapulting Macbeth to his fate as breathtakingly as a rollercoaster.

This terminal spasm of the tragedy seems especially relevant at the moment, for it bears an uncanny resemblance to the psychedelic world of advertising, at which we've just been looking. Little in contemporary life so fully captures the awesome, horrifying thrill of *Macbeth* as advertising does. In both we run smack into a crazy kaleidoscope of images, a surrealist compounding of furious phantasms and the incredible come true. Birnam Wood walks; give it the tyrant's blood. The stomach talks; give it Alka-Seltzer. Advertisers machine-gunning jet-age plastic are merely aping the Bard as he richly peppers us with engrams of a different sort. In either case, our minds stagger under the burden of vivid, pulsating images. Above all, the tragedy of *Macbeth* and the drama of advertising seem both to convey the same dominant theme: Someone (Macbeth, us) is being hustled pell mell to a future that has doom written all over it.

What is advertising, its critics ask, but the visual cause and symbol of American materialism? The worship of the almighty dollar must have a liturgy, as every good cultus does. Advertising stages that liturgy, with rubrics spelled out by Madison Avenue. As *Time* magazine put it, ". . . commercials obviously represent the American materialist vision of the good life—all the shiny possessions and luxuries that people want, or are supposed to want." [1]

What *Time* is saying is that Americans worship Mammon, and advertising is proof positive of that idolatry. Want to know what we love? Look at the commercials. Thus, say the critics, we are sliding headlong to our destruction down the greased pole of materialism. Like Macbeth we are achieving our vainglorious, sensual ambitions by murdering good taste and those spiritual sensibilities so evident in other countries. (The critics don't specify which countries.) Our consciences, bridling at our sacrifice of quality of life for style of life, leave us no peace. We have murdered sleep, and neither pills nor security blankets will restore it to us. Our folly is bringing on a wholesale reenactment of Macbeth's mindless (or headless) finish at the hands of nemesis Macduff. One can only hope that television and the newspapers, like Shakespeare, will have the good taste to keep our cultural decapitation off-stage.

What are we to make of all this? Are we Americans a nation of fornicators, as the Old Testament phrases it? Are we really shacking up in those dreadful "high places" with two little sluts named Avaritia and Cupiditas? Do we worship the almighty dollar? Modern pundits, with more gall than Burke, do not hesitate to draw up a bill of indict-

---

[1] *Time*, July 22, 1968, p. 55.

ment against an entire people—us—charging that we are base materialists lovestruck by golden calves.

I should like to say here that American materialism is a myth. If there is one myth that deserves at long last to be laid to rest it is *the myth of American materialism*. It won't be an easy interment, not in this era of almost masochistic *mea culpas*. But let us undertake it all the same

Arguments supporting the myth run in familiar paths. We are materialists because we have so much money. Nonsense! It happens that we have evolved an economic system in which workmen are amply rewarded in the best way the system knows, with money. But work deserves a reward. And what ought we to substitute for the generous salaries? Should employers keep wages low and for bonuses bestow ribbons with "Comrade Hard Worker" on them, or award us a benison of speeches, or inscribe our names on grand proletarian monuments, one per factory? Are we materialists because we spend a lot of money. Not at all. Our spending may be evidence of our spendthrift or prodigal nature, but not of materialism. And I had been under the impression, come to think of it, that one of the aims of the United Nations was to lift the standard of life in other countries to a level more closely approximating our own, if not equaling it. Is the U.N. bent on converting the world into a nest of materialists?

You miss the point, cries the critic. Americans are materialists because they judge their fellowman on the basis of his wealth. Well, some of us do at times. But that is a rather universal trait, reaching even to England, bastion of the blooded aristocracy, as H. C. Allen observed some years ago.[2] The monetary rewards attaching to various careers

[2] H. C. Allen, *The Anglo-American Predicament* (New York: Macmillan, 1960). See also Allen's "The Myth of American Materialism" in *The Month*, October, 1962, p. 211.

are not so much a reflection of the value we place on those careers but are more often the result of a simpler law: supply and demand. Give the people a popular product, and they'll make you a millionaire. A trumpet player with an ear for a nifty arrangement rises in a few years from movie extra to head of a $30 million enterprise. We term him "a success." Is it an improvement to term a man a success because his father is the Prince of Wales? We honor Herb Alpert for his musical expertise; we do not thereby make any judgment of his personal worth. The system enriches him materially; his personal enrichment must come from within himself. Adults judge the two things separately.

Well, concludes the critic, you can't deny that America has always reverenced the tycoon more than the politician or statesman. As a result, your best men have gone into business instead of leading your nation. How can you explain that other than by materialism? In the first place, as I have already pointed out, the fact that tycoons make a lot of money is no sign that we reverence them. The dubious legacy of men like Gould, Vanderbilt, and Harriman gives evidence, not of reverence, but of a suspicion on our part of anyone with a fortune. We wonder how he got it and how he is using it. And in the second place, there is no way of proving that our "best men" have preferred business to politics. In fact, on the basis of the monetary rewards of the two fields, which the critics cite, the very opposite would seem to be the case. Men who are devoted above all to the pursuit of money (and who are not, therefore, our best men by a long shot) will choose the more lucrative field. We should expect the more spiritual man to select a career, like politics, whose rewards are, in comparison with the tycoon's, meager. A system like that, I should think, is a rather fortunate one.

Moaning that advertising reflects a "materialist vision" of America as a collection of money-hungry slobs is hopelessly naive. It is like condemning railroads for showing American cities to their patrons as oases of junkyards, rusty sidings, ding-dong crossing signals, freight yards, and the iterative arcs of little red lanterns. As it happens, railroad rights-of-way happen to go through that portion of the cityscape. And as it happens, advertising of its nature happens to dote on manufactured goods. If we should demand that the railroad fly high above the material world, all the junkyards would of course disappear—but so would the railroad. The same thing is true of advertising. Ads are paeans to material objects, but economies deal in the production of material objects. I have not lately seen an advertisement that offers the reader "summer bargains on the four cardinal virtues, individually packaged, with any one of the three theological virtues thrown in free to the first fifty readers who answer the ad." Courage, nobility, patriotism, insight, self-sacrifice, and love of God are not advertised on television, or anywhere else. But they may well be, I suppose, just as soon as *Time* tells industry how to manufacture them.

By stimulating sales, advertising creates a demand for more jobs, puts more people to work, and thus spreads the "good life" of material abundance around. But the "good life" is not an evil thing. It is not a lewd succubus leeching us of our virtue. It is rather a necessary base for achievement of any sort, whether intellectual, artistic, or spiritual. The head hunters down in savage Papua, all decked out in jungle cosmetics and cassowary feathers, are much too concerned about their next meal to produce fine art or to add to the fund of human knowledge. If advertising sells more soap it gives more jobs to soap-makers. This is not an unworthy goal, unless perchance one feels that the odor of sanctity and the odor of fetid armpits are inseparable—a thesis that has not found favor except in a few monastic manuals now out of date.

"Advertising obviously represents the American materialist vision of the good life." Poppycock! It does no such thing. Rather it displays for our perusal and acceptance the whole gamut of goods that you and I make a living by producing. In the process we enrich ourselves and others. Our standard of living is high, so high that it irks the very devil out of less affluent societies. But that standard, we should remember, is in the words of Belgian economist Jules de Mey, S.J., "the result of enormous toil and sacrifice." After all, we could be out snoozing under a cool mulberry bush. Let me repeat that: Our standard of living is the product of hard work and talent liberally expended. Neither is frowned upon by the Scriptures. In fact, Christ urges us to use our talents, to work by the sweat of our brows. If there is a spiritual reward, as we hope, He will confer it. Our economy makes no pretense of usurping His role. It pays us in another way, the only way it can.

I said that American materialism is a myth. I don't mean to say that the charge is wholly without foundation. A myth, as we know, is not a fairy tale. The story in Genesis about Adam and Eve may be a myth, but that does not mean it is the imaginary elucubration of some Iron Age Grimm brother. It is a myth because it presents a *truth* in symbolic language (Ernst Cassirer). What truth? A couple (whatever their names) enjoyed a peculiar intimacy with God which they lost by a free and deliberate rejection of His will. The loss damaged not only themselves but all of us who are their descendants. The pedagogical tricks or symbolic language of the narrator (the garden, snake, angel with flaming sword, and evening walks in the garden with God) are the ornamental framework in which the truth is presented. We can dispense with the framework; we cannot dispense with the truth it contains. The Church enables us to distinguish one from the other.

When I say, then, that American materialism is a myth, I mean that some, not all, Americans are materialists. Probably a minority. This minority reveals its oblique sense of values by the way it spends its money. To cite an example. A writer just the other day received about three quarters of a million dollars in advance royalties for his new novel which details the ignoble "sexploits" (apologies to Walter Winchell) of a thoroughly mixed up young man. How many other novels are best sellers whose heroes are nothing more than Marco Polos of the perineum, tediously exploring, gaping, and making topographical charts? Evidently a considerable number of us book buyers are either awfully ignorant, awfully curious, or awfully venereal. But not our whole society. If it is not altogether perfect, it is not totally corrupt either. One only hopes that some degree of sanity can begin to qualify our judgments of America and her people.

No, everything in our nation is not perfect, far from it. But I have discovered nothing elsewhere that tempts me to set sail from our shores. Our government is officially areligious. It is required by the Constitution to treat all religions alike—not to *mistreat* them all alike, as the enemies of the parochial schools and others claim. Our society admits of no aristocracy of blood, but one only of sweat and genius, Jefferson's "natural aristocracy." The axiomatic problem in such a system is the difficulty of establishing a uniform code of behavior by which good men and bad men (and the rest of us, too) can be judged. We have no *grande noblesse* as in France, no Established Church as in England to tell us how to conduct ourselves in public life. But I doubt if we want either. What we do have is the individual conscience, informed and inspired by a free and independent Church, which acts as our guide to responsibility and to heroism. And the Church, to the best of my knowledge, is still reminding us constantly from the pulpit:

Do not store up for yourselves treasures on earth, where rust and moth consume, and where thieves may break in and steal. But store up for yourselves treasures in heaven, where neither rust nor moth consumes, nor thieves break in to steal. For where your treasure is, there your heart will be as well. (Mt 6:19-21)